You Can't Judge
a Cop by Its Cover

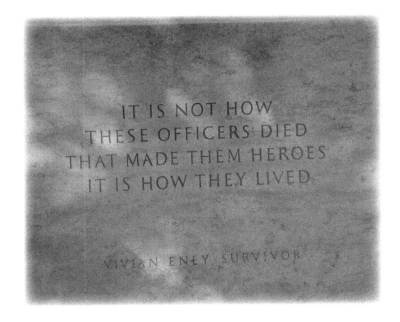

Rodney LeMond

PAGE PUBLISHING, INC.
Conneaut Lake, PA

First originally published by Page Publishing 2021

ISBN 978-1-6624-3072-5 (pbk)
ISBN 978-1-6624-3073-2 (digital)

Printed in the United States of America

LET ME START out my story by saying that police work was a very challenging, stressful, dangerous, and unappreciated yet rewarding career for me. If it was all those things rolled up in to one, it must sound highly confusing to you. And how could it give you all the negative feelings yet still be rewarding? Well, as you read on, I am hoping to be able to make it all clear.

I know that a great deal of the American people lost respect for law enforcement in this country. I think that a lot of that comes from influence by politicians, the media, radical groups, and also the fact that they have a true lack of understanding and knowledge as to what their police officers face on a daily basis. And I am not just referring to state and local police, I am referring to an understanding as to what our Federal agents face as well.

There is a Law Enforcement Memorial in Washington, DC. It is 304 feet long and has the names of 21,000 fallen officers on it, killed in the line of duty. And names are added annually. There are different inscriptions on the memorial, these words:

> The wicked flee when no man pursueth; but the righteous as bold as a lion.
> —Proverbs 28:1

> Carved on these walls is the story of America, of a continuing quest to preserve both democracy and decency, and to protect a national treasure that we call the American dream.
> —President George H. W. Bush

It is not how these officers died that made them heroes, it is how they lived.

—Vivian Eney, survivor

Think of the true meaning behind those inscriptions. And as you are thinking, ask yourselves, do we really want to do away with cops?

As you get into the story, you will also learn that not all cops are perfect nor would I ever say that they were. Just as in any profession, people make mistakes. Police work can definitely change a person and not always for the better. The stresses of the job can sometimes take its toll. Cops are human beings and not programmable machines. That is why their behavior needs to be closely monitored by their agencies throughout their careers.

I also feel that we have become a nation full of certain people that don't believe in the laws of this country and would very much like to do away with them. They are those that continue to stir up chaos and threaten the lives of good law-abiding Americans. A nation without laws cannot survive. That's why I felt the need to share my feelings with you and my experiences.

As you read on, I will talk a lot about myself and my twenty-eight-year career in police work, and why do I feel the need to write about myself, and why would anyone be interested in my story?

Well, it is because my life has been pretty unique; however, I am not writing just about me, I am writing about all law enforcement officers, men and women. I am just using my life as an example. I have never liked the stereotyping of officers that occurs, and I want you to understand that not all officers are the same. I have been part of highly unusual events that seemed to have occurred time and time again, and it took me years to realize why. I believe it was because it came from a higher calling. So, please read on and make a determination for yourself.

I have heard the phrase on several occasions, "Law enforcement officers were peacekeepers, angels of God." I believe that I was pushed towards police work for some reason that I have never been able to explain.

There is something else that I don't think that the general public knows about police work. I want to enlighten you as to what it takes to become a cop and what it takes to remain a cop.

First of all, I had to apply for a position. You were required to have a high school diploma or equivalent or preferably a college degree. I could not have ever been charged with a felony, I could not have ever had any type of prior drug usage, I could not have ever been charged with a misdemeanor that involved moral turpitude. A lengthy background investigation was done on me. I could not have any visible tattoos. Investigators spoke to my neighbors. I had to take a lengthy psychological exam, two parts, written and oral with a psychologist. I had to go before an oral review board. I had to take a written test and achieve a passing score of at least 85 percent. I had to take a physical agility test doing sit-ups, push-ups, chin-ups, and a lengthy swim test. I had to run a mile and a half in less than twelve minutes. I had to run an obstacle course, part of it dragging a one-hundred-fifty-pound dummy. I had to attend a police academy that lasted seven months. You had quarterly written tests; if you failed anyone of them, you were out. You had to attend the firing range regularly throughout the academy and pass qualifications shooting under the most stressful situations that the range instructors could put on you. You had physical fitness testing, training, and defensive tactics. You had weapon retention training. You had collision avoidance training driving at high speed on a road course and a decision-making driving. And all this was just to get a job as a cop. You also had to take and pass the state exam.

Once you got hired, you had to go through a field training program where you would ride with a field training officer. This lasted on average about nine weeks. The training officers would place a great deal of pressure on you during the training and grade you on how you would deal with stressful situations. Some trainees would talk about how they would become so stressed out that they would go home and vomit at night.

Your first year, you were considered an-at-will deputy, and you could be terminated without any means of contesting the termination. Continual training would be required throughout your career.

Such as human diversity training, counseling, and communications training, so much more training and retraining it is difficult to list it all. But it would be thousands of hours. I hope you get an idea of how extensive it was.

There was a machine called a FATS machine that stood for firearms training simulator. It was a machine that was very realistic with live scenarios of decision-making events. You would be tested as to shoot or don't shoot situations. We would have to train on it regularly.

When the Naval Training Center closed in Orlando, Florida, we were afforded the opportunity to use the facility for training purposes. It was like having your own private city. We would use guns with Simunition ammo, which is training ammunition or paint balls. We could train doing mock bank robberies, armed traffic stops, and several other work-related scenarios.

Well, here it is, my beginning. I started early on in life with no father figure due to losing my dad to that dreaded disease, cancer. During the trying times while my dad was hospitalized for two years fighting for his life, my mom worked at a fast-food restaurant in an effort to keep food on our table. It was a minimum-wage job and just wasn't enough income to support six children, so she was forced to apply for Welfare. I remember us getting large cans of peanut butter that had so much oil on top you would have to scoop it out with a spoon prior to being able to make a sandwich. I also remember us getting large blocks of cheese. It was really tough times.

When I was eight years old, I remember the hospital that my dad was in allowed him to come home. It was for only a few days, and it was a week before my ninth birthday. I would lay in my bed at night and listen to my dad cry because he was in excruciating pain. He would tell my mom that he didn't want to die. I remember looking through the opening in my bedroom door and seeing my mom carrying blood-soaked sheets from their bedroom. The blood was from cancerous tumors on my dad's body that were breaking. It was an unimaginable memory that I can never forget. My dad had to return to the hospital but before he left, he kissed me and gave me a silver dollar. My dad never kissed me. He was always a masculine man. My dad died the day before my ninth birthday while he was back in the hospital.

From the age of ten to the age of fourteen, I had a stepfather. I won't say he raised me because he was a very physically abusive man towards my mom, myself, and the rest of my family. He didn't have much time for the kids, but he had plenty of time for other women and bars. He was definitely no role model. Several of my friends were experiencing the physical abuse from stepfathers as well.

I remember when I was about ten years old (probably the year 1965), I was going with my stepfather to Salisbury, North Carolina to visit his sister. We were at her home, and it was just getting dark. I looked out of the front window of her living room and saw a fire forming in a field across the street. It was in the shape of a cross and something like I had never seen before. I asked my stepfather's sister what it was, and she said, "Oh, it was just the Klan." She said that a black family had moved across the tracks and that the Klan was going to run them out. The Klan? What was the Klan? I had no clue. Then I saw numbers of people wearing what looked like white sheets and white hoods gathering around the cross as if to be sending some kind of intimidating message. I was scared to death, and everyone else there acted as if it was just a normal thing. Their explanation was that the Klan was bigger than they were, and there was nothing that they could do about it. It appeared to me that this was some kind of normal thing at that time in that area. That was one of the many horrible things that this man exposed me to during my childhood. Even at the age of ten, I knew that all people were equal, and I couldn't believe what I had just witnessed.

After I returned home, I tried to educate myself more about the Ku Klux Klan, and in my opinion, I felt that they were uneducated, radical white supremacists. They posed as being a part of a white supremacy, and they hated blacks. Yet they were neo-Nazi. Neo-Nazi supported the killing of millions of Jewish people whom were white. That just proved how intelligent they were.

At fourteen, I was pretty much on my own, and considering the man that my stepfather was, that wasn't a bad thing. Later after my brother and I grew, my stepdad couldn't get away with the things he had been doing because we were no longer afraid of him. And when I say the things he had gotten away with, let me give you just one example. I reflected back to a morning that I was to be awakened by my mom. She walked into my bedroom, I think I was around twelve years old, and when I looked at her, I didn't recognize her. Her eyes were swollen shut, she had metal rods up her nose, and her face was bruised badly. She told me that she and my stepfather were in a bad car accident. She never said in what car, and our car had no damage. A couple of years later, I found out that my stepfather had punched her in the face and broke her nose the evening before she entered my bedroom. She had just returned from the hospital emergency room. Then on another occasion, we were all outside of our home enjoying the nice weather. My mom was sitting in a lawn chair and my stepfather was sitting next to her. I watched him stand up and punch her in the face and knock her out of the chair. Then he dragged her by her hair as she was bleeding badly into the house. I was still very young and unable to do anything about it. Why he was never charged criminally for the horrible abuse was beyond me.

I had begun to have my little encounters with the law. Nothing serious. I took a minibike that didn't belong to me. I got put on probation, and that was when I met a savior that entered my life. He was a corporal with the local police department, and he was my probation officer. He took me and other troubled kids to major league baseball games and became a true role model. I think that was when I began to take a strong interest in police work. Shortly after turning fourteen, my stepdad came out looking for me one evening when I was with some friends. He began to beat me with his fists like I was a grown man right in front of them. He was not a small man. He was about 6'2" and over 200 pounds. To this day, I don't recall what I may have done to ever deserve that. I became tired of the abuse and never having anything. And as I said earlier, we grew up pretty poor. I also remember that we had one bicycle for all six kids to share. It was a twenty-six-inch bike, so I would have to lean it against the fence then get up on the fence to get on it.

I also remember wanting to become a Cub Scout. We couldn't afford a uniform, so a friend gave me his old one. It was faded blue and pretty worn. I was so embarrassed going to meetings and seeing the dark blue new uniforms all the other kids were wearing and seeing how different I looked. My mom was finally able to get up the ten dollars that a new uniform cost, and she bought me one. I knew how much of a struggle she had with five other kids to provide for, but some way she did it. My dad was deathly sick at the time and permanently hospitalized.

I learned to fight at a very young age due to having to defend myself regularly from my stepdad and kids from the neighborhood. I took up boxing at the YMCA, and I got pretty good and was fighting in competitive bouts. But it was beginning to become an important learning experience for me, and I started to see that it was not the life I wanted to lead. I began lifting weights and continued to train in boxing in an attempt to get stronger because I knew my stepfather would continue his abuse if he wasn't stopped.

My brother and I grew older and wiser and were no longer going to take my stepfather's insane behavior. My brother enlisted in the army, and we were having a going-away party for him. My stepfather and a couple of his friends waited until all the guests at the party left, including me, and all of them beat my brother up pretty badly. I was furious when I heard what happened. My stepfather needed to pay for all he had been doing.

My brother returned home from the army before he was going to be shipped off overseas. I was visiting at my mom's house with my wife and two small sons. I looked out the window and saw my brother walking towards the house in uniform. He was coming to surprise my mom. When he got into the house, my stepfather started in on him immediately. He told my brother to leave his house. My brother said, "Your house? My dad payed for this house." My stepfather told my brother to step outside, and they did. I watched as my brother was bending over to unlace his boots, and I watched my stepfather kick him in the face.

My wife kept saying to me, "I know what you are thinking, and I am telling you, don't get involved."

I said, "The hell with that, I have experienced enough of this."

I went outside, and my stepfather and my brother were fighting. I grabbed my stepfather and punched him in the face, knocking him to the ground. I had him down and continued to punch him in the face. It was like all my anger towards him was being released all at once. His friend, J.R., was there visiting as well, and he came outside. My stepfather kept yelling, "J.R., get him off of me!"

I held my stepfather by the neck and looked at J.R. and said, "Yeah, you come and get some of this too."

J.R. said, "No, this is family, I am not getting involved."

That was a good idea on his part. I had a lot of built-up anger and enough left to go around. Especially after knowing that J.R. was one of the ones that helped beat my brother before he left for the army.

Being the nasty, dirty, and sneaky person my stepfather was, he wasn't finished. I was working for a trucking company and working overtime to make extra money on the weekends. I got off work on a Saturday and went to the sports bar located just a few blocks away from the warehouse I was driving truck out of. Me and a few friends wanted to stop and watch the Detroit Tiger baseball game. While I was there watching the game, my stepfather was calling the barmaid that he knew that worked at the bar and kept asking her if I was there and asked how long I had been there. After about an hour or so, he came walking in the bar and right up to me. I stood up immediately because I knew we were on bad terms and I knew he was there to fight.

He put his hands out and said, "Son, son, I just came to talk."

I sat back down, and the way I was sitting, I had my back against the wall with a table on each side of me.

My step father said, "It isn't you I have a problem with, it is your brother."

I said to him, "If you have a problem with my brother, you have a problem with me."

He said "No, son, I love you" then he grabbed a beer bottle and broke it over my head.

I got dizzy, but I didn't lose consciousness. I could feel the blood running down my face, and I got enraged. I leaned back and kicked him over the table in front of me. I grabbed him by the throat and began choking him while I was trying to regain my senses after being hit by the bottle. Two guys grabbed me and pulled me off him, and he ran out of the bar. How could I have been so stupid as to fall for his dirty tactics. He was nothing but a coward.

As a result of mine and my brother's actions, my mom also lost her fear of him, and she finally got the courage to divorce him. But in the process, he had taken the home that my dad's money paid for, and my mom had pretty much been left with nothing. Thankfully, she had six loving children that continued to care for her all these years.

I think back to when my dad was well and how much he loved baseball. He would take us to the park and pitch to us. He still made the effort even when he started getting sick in his early thirties. He loved the game that much. After his death, my mom had him buried at a cemetery behind baseball fields. I had visited him there several times, and the ball fields still remain out front.

When I saw the movie *Field of Dreams* for the first time, it really touched me. There was a scene in the movie when actor Kevin Costner sees his father on the field wearing catcher's gear. It is actually his father's ghost. Kevin Costner says to his father, "Hey, Dad, you want to have a catch?" The actor that played the role of his father, Dwier Brown, looked so much to me like my dad it was hard to believe.

And just the fact that he never got to play catch with his dad when he was alive reminds me of my situation. It still gets to me every time I see the movie. I really want to visit the actual *Field of Dreams*, who knows what I may find.

I have shared all these experiences in an effort to make a point about police officers. You see, after becoming a cop, I attended a proffer one day that we were holding for one of the defendants in a high-profile drug case that I had worked. A proffer is when a person in a federal criminal case cooperates in an effort to get leniency for their actions. On that particular day, there was a high-dollar defense attorney present representing the defendant. The defendant in a proffer is required to be totally truthful or all bets are off. Well, I knew that in this case, the defendant was not being truthful, and I called him on it. The defense attorney accused me of being born with a silver spoon in my mouth, and he said that I would never know what it was like to want for anything. Well, needless to say, that didn't exactly set right with me, and to say the least, I set him and the record straight. So, I am not bringing up my childhood looking for sympathy, I am just trying to make it clear that police officers come from all walks of life.

It was then that I knew that I wanted to do something or be somebody that would make all my family proud. I had been growing up in the suburbs of Detroit, Michigan, and at the time, the economy was pretty bad. I found one of my earlier jobs at the Heick bullet company making bullets for the Detroit Police Department, and that was going nowhere. I had to say I was eighteen just so I could work to feed the family. It was a very low-paying job and was just not paying the bills. I couldn't afford college, so I just had to do what I had to do.

I then ventured into the auto industry and started working for Chrysler Corporation. It was troubled times, and I was laid off regularly. And it was again not paying the bills. However, while I was employed there, I was able to go through training for skilled trades, and that would help me with a lot of things later on in life. You see, I was trying to learn everything that I could about as much as I could. That helped in saving a great deal of money by me being able to fix and repair things without having to pay somebody else. I also enrolled in a motorcycle mechanics school and learned how to fix and build motorcycles. After getting certified, I got a part-time job at a local Harley Davidson dealership in Michigan assembling the new motorcycles when they arrived. It was actually a second job.

I started a side business working out of my garage at home, repairing and rebuilding motorcycles to generate additional income for the household. I bought a couple of wrecked Harleys and put them back together and sold them as well. I was always trying to do something to give my family all that I could during such an uncertain economy.

I was fortunate enough to be able to work at my brother-in-law's father's hydraulic company during the laid-off periods at Chrysler's, and it was there that I met a man that I believe became another one of my saviors. And the reason I say savior is because I would find he was one, and there would be many more to come throughout my life. People that for some unknown reason enter your life and have a huge impact on you. Not always necessarily by helping you but also just by having an influence on you.

Up until then, I never had anybody offer me help or see any potential in me. He was a professional man and ran his servo valve business in a leased area of the shop. He took an interest in my abilities and work ethics, and he offered to pay to put me through school to become a certified servo valve technician. There was good money to be made in the hydraulic business; however, there was a force pushing me towards something else. I was extremely appreciative concerning his offer, but I told him about a strong interest I had of becoming a police officer. I told him how I somehow wanted to make a difference in other's lives. I know that a lot of cop's early on in their careers probably felt the same way, and I sure hope that it held true and that throughout my career I did make a positive difference. He understood and said that he knew someone at the Wayne County Sheriff's Department in Detroit, Michigan, and that he could get me an interview.

I took him up on that offer and was able to land the job as a deputy sheriff working in the Jail Division in downtown Detroit.

Once again, due to the bad economy and the sheriff not being able to get his budget, I was being laid off regularly. In Wayne County, you could work the road one day and be in the jail the next, just depending on manpower, or you may not be working at all. It wasn't looking good for me to ever be able to land the job I was pursuing. I would like to point out something that makes me laugh today. It was something that a lieutenant with the sheriff's department said to me. He told me that I didn't have the makings of a good deputy sheriff. I don't know what he based his opinion on, but what if I would have listened to him and gave up on the idea? Never give up on your dreams, and never let anyone tell you that you can't do something. And as you read on, you will see how wrong I believe people can be about another person. You will see that I had a very successful career, and I feel that I served the people honorably.

I served nearly twenty-seven years with the Orange County Sheriff's Office alone and never received so much as a verbal reprimand. I was never disciplined for anything. I was highly decorated and received the agency's highest award and numerous other awards from the sheriff's office, as well as outside agencies.

I was now forced to get into the trucking business to try to keep food on the table. I think I leaned towards that type of work because my dad was a trucker (owner/operator). I had a family to care for, and unlike a lot of people today, I surely didn't want to have to be dependent on the government to care for me. Even through the hardships, I was not willing to give up. I remained creative and somehow managed to earn money. I taught myself how to operate big trucks and had to tell my first employer that hired me to drive a tractor-trailer that I had experience. They believed me, and they gave me the job. I hated to mislead them, but I needed work to support my family. I was fortunate that they asked the driver that was leaving the company to stay on and ride with me for two weeks. Thank goodness they did because I confided in him and told him that I had no experience. I asked him to please have faith in me and that if he was not satisfied with my driving abilities by the end of the two weeks, I would go and tell my employer myself about not being able to drive the big truck. Well, he agreed, and he showed me all that he knew about trucking, and lo and behold, I was whipping that truck around as if I was born driving it. Was this another person that entered my life for some unknown reason, another savior? That job gave me my start, and I was able to keep getting better paying jobs in the industry as a result.

And as I was telling you earlier on about something being unique about my life, well unusual things were continuing to happen. I will share another example. I was driving truck one day on I-94 in Belleville, Michigan, it was snowing very hard, and the roads were awful. Visibility was bad, and traffic was heavy. I somehow got my truck stuck along the service drive off I-94 that led to the Lemon Tree Apartments. I set out my emergency triangles and was doing everything that I could to dig myself out. Traffic was going by me at high rates of speed and actually damaged some of the triangles. There was not much sympathy being shown by anybody. Then out of nowhere, a new Ford conversion van pulled up behind me and stopped. This was in the mid to late '70s and in the heart of winter.

A young man got out of the van and ran up to where I was at under the rear wheels of the truck trying to dig the truck out. I will never forget him. He was wearing old blue jeans, new gloves, new boots, a fleece-lined jean jacket, and a flapper-type hat. He had bushy blonde hair coming out from under the hat, and he was full of energy. He began digging with his hands rapidly under the truck and told me to get into the driver's seat and try rocking the truck. When I got behind the wheel, it dawned on me. This guy was my favorite Detroit Tiger. I have been a huge Tiger fan since my childhood, and this was actually Detroit Tiger pitcher Mark "the Bird" Fidrych under my truck trying to dig me out with his hands. He told me to try rocking the truck, and I looked back and down at him, and I said, "You're the Bird" and he looked up at me and he smiled, and he put his finger up to his mouth, gesturing for me to be quiet. I smiled at him and said, "Whatever you do, don't hurt your pitching hand." What a class act he was!

Out of all the people to stop and help, it was him, a popular Major League Baseball player getting out in the cold and risking his safety just to help me. I can't even describe how I felt that day. Well, he did help get me unstuck, and I couldn't thank him enough. We talked for a bit, and he told me that he lived at the Lemon Tree Apartments and that he was on his way home. He also said that his family owned a trucking company in his home state of Massachusetts, so he could relate to the situation I was in. He gave me his autograph on a piece of paper and his address. He said that I could stop by some time. I asked if I could bring a friend, and he said sure.

I told my friend Jimmy about my experience, and naturally he didn't believe me. So, I took him to Mark Fidrych's apartment. I knocked at the door, and Mark's roommate answered. Mark wasn't at home, but Jimmy actually got to meet the roommate, Detroit Tiger outfielder Ben Oglivie. It was still such a thrill for both of us even though Mark "the Bird" Fidrych wasn't home. Ben Oglivie was so kind and friendly. He, too, was a class act. My only regret is that somehow the autograph Mark gave me was lost. Mark is gone now, and I later learned that his cause of death was due to an accident involving him working under a family-owned Mack truck in his hometown of Worcester, Massachusetts. Mark was obviously a family man that never let his fame go to his head. He died way too soon at age fifty-four. He is truly missed by many. But how ironic was this experience for me. And do we chalk it up to coincidence? I don't think so, but it is my belief that it all happened for a reason.

I went on to work for a few different companies and then eventually was able to buy my own truck and go into business for myself as an owner-operator. I found that it was not a glamorous life like shown on television; however, I was making some money. I found myself away from home quite a bit and was not happy about that, but I had to provide. If the truck wasn't moving, it wasn't making money. For some reason, the authorities thought that truckers made a lot of money, and they always had their hand in your pockets either by fining you for some trivial things or forcing you to pay high road use taxes, the high cost of plates and insurance, and the high cost of fuel made things difficult. It started out good; I was staying busy, but then again, something went wrong. I was unable to get loads in or out of Michigan, and running empty to get to and from home for hundreds of miles was very costly. It was really becoming a struggle to make ends meet.

I was always so close at getting a break; however, it just never seemed to happen. One example was during a delivery to Ford Motor Company in Woodhaven, Michigan, I met a representative of Ford's who was extremely pleased with my work. He was going to offer me a contract for an exclusive use run to and from Missouri. The pay would have been excellent. We were supposed to set up the contract during my next trip back. When I met with him, he apologized and said that because of poor sales in the auto industry, they were cutting back production, so basically, no deal. It was again another setback.

I just refused to give up. Then another savior entered my life. I met a woman that was in the trucking business that had a contract with General Motors. She was offering to buy my truck and put it to work but not with me in it. This seemed to be kind of a slap in the face; however, it turned out to be some sort of saving grace. By her doing this, it would again give me the opportunity to pursue the job I hoped for. I sold the truck to her, and this gave me some money to work with and no more pressure from the business. I was beginning to learn that things do happen for a reason.

Now it was time to pack up and look for opportunity, so I decided to be Florida bound. This is where I have to tell you to not listen to all advice from others. They truly don't always have the answers. I was told by many that I was making a huge mistake and to not set out to do what I was about to do. I still had my family's best interest at heart and was determined to give them the best life I possibly could, so I made my decision after talking it over with them to go. When I left, I had an interview set up to meet with staff at Raiford Prison in Starke, Florida, where I would possibly be offered a position. Well, I left early and went to the Orlando, Florida, area to visit with my brother first who had recently moved to that location from Michigan. Thank goodness I did. I immediately started a job transporting boats for Regal Marine out of Orlando and was making money. The company was so generous they even loaded me to Dearborn, Michigan, and told me that since I would be coming back empty, I could use the truck to move all my furniture and belongings back down. My family would fly down after that.

Once I got settled in an apartment, I sent for them. I later saw an ad for positions with the Orange County Sheriff's Office in corrections. It appeared that they were hiring corrections officers, so I did some homework and looked into the agency's background. They had a real good reputation as one of the best law enforcement agencies in the state.

Could this be the opportunity that I had been hoping for? Did I really want to work at Raiford, home of the electric chair knowing that there was no other possibility of being anything other than a prison guard? And please don't mistake what I said. Prison guards play a vital role in our society, and I would never say anything negative about their position. I have the utmost respect for them. I just had a plan that had been put into motion, and it had to be followed through. The Orange County Sheriff's Office had much more possibilities for a better future and the chance for me to pursue real police work. So, I applied for the position of corrections officer in hopes to establish myself and get my foot in the door. And now yet another savior was about to enter my life. I believe that God has a purpose for us all. I also feel that I was sent to Florida for a reason, and that was to somehow do God's work. And soon I would explain what led me to believe all this. Ironic things began to start happening. Things that I have no explanation for.

During the interview process, one of the people on the interview board was a man by the name of Dwayne Rutledge. I didn't know it at the time I was being interviewed, but Dwayne Rutledge had previously been the warden at Raiford Prison and just left to come to work as the Director of the Orange County Jail. Was that coincidence or was that fate? He said to me that I would be making a huge mistake by taking the job at Raiford. When I was leaving the interview, Mr. Rutledge stopped me and referred to me as a self-made man. What led him to believe that was that he knew about my upbringing and how I had to succeed without help. He then said to me that he didn't feel that I ever had a bad day. I smiled and said, "Not if I can help it."

That man would become another inspiration to me because he was one of the first to show that he believed in me in doing police work, and he proved it later on by giving me so much responsibility at the ripe old age of twenty-six. By his putting his trust in me the way that he did, I had something more to prove. I would never let him down. He also gave me the integrity, work ethic, and loyalty that I always hoped to show to others throughout the course of my life. My only regret was that I was never able to sincerely thank that man for the positive impact that he had on my life. He passed away before I got the chance. I was able to advance to the rank of sergeant in two years and was the supervisor of the midnight shift in charge of the entire facility. At the time, we housed nearly two thousand inmates, and I was in charge of approximately sixty corrections officers.

During my time on the shift, on one occasion, two seasoned officers came to me and laughingly said that they had overheard a conversation where a male inmate was talking to his girlfriend on the telephone and she told the inmate that he had been replaced by another man. The officers found it funny. I immediately had some type of urge to go to the inmate as if God had spoken. I told the officers to take me to him immediately. When we got to him, he had already hung himself. We cut him down and was able to save his life. I was honored by the sheriff's office for my decisive actions in saving a human being. This would only become the beginning of being in the right place at the right time for me after entering police work. More and more spiritual things were about to happen.

Another incident in the jail that occurred under my watch was when another male inmate was told by his wife over the phone that she could no longer go on without him. She shot herself in the head as she was speaking to him. The inmate was completely out of control, and yet I was able to talk him down without having to be physical. I sat with him in a private interview room and consoled him, letting him know that I had checked and that everything possible was being done for his wife. He was a big man, and if he wanted to, he could have inflicted a whole lot of damage. I assured him that I was doing everything that I could to get him a hardship release. I had put in a request for the chaplain; however, the chaplain wouldn't respond until seven hours later.

I sat with the inmate for that seven hours and was able to keep him calm and under control until the chaplain arrived. God must have been at my side every step of the way, and he provided me with the right things to say. A seasoned supervisor, whom at the time did not have a lot of respect for me because I had been given more responsibility than him and because of my age and I was given more authority than he, later came to me to tell me how wrong he was about me. He told me that he observed me handle things in a way that a thirty-year veteran would not have been able to handle. He said that he was highly impressed. Maybe it was because I had matured before my time having to start out so early in life. Or maybe it was because of my sincere intent when dealing with people.

It was now becoming apparent to me that my work was done in the jail, and it was now time to move on. I feel that this course of action was again put into place for me. I don't know that it was something I did on my own. It is hard to explain. Did you ever have something just begin to unfold in your life somewhat wanting it but not really pushing for it? And then you merely see it transform. Well, that was what I was seeing.

I enrolled in the police academy to get my Florida state standards and certification in law enforcement. It was not easy. I had already completed one academy and now another one? I had to work a full-time job and attend the academy weekdays and on Saturdays for seven months. This move upset the director, Dwayne Rutledge, and he was going to let me know it. He put me on the midnight shift, knowing that I would have to go to the academy during the day. I was not getting a great deal of sleep and losing a lot of weight due to the strenuous exercise and running eight miles a day. One of my instructors in the academy wore a shirt that had Dr. Pain printed on the front of it. And believe me, there was a great deal of pain going on. The director would comment about how bad he thought I looked. I think he was hoping I would drop out and stay in the jail. There was no way I was going to do that. When I set my mind to something, I saw it through.

I don't blame him or hold any ill feelings towards him. I now know that he saw something in me, and he was looking at me advancing to the top in corrections. I think he was hurt more than angry.

Well, in my police academy, I was elected class president and was basically responsible for getting all the recruits to tow the line and make it through to graduation. This was another huge task and responsibility placed on my shoulders. I saw it through, and I feel I earned respect from the class, each of the instructors, and the class coordinator. I graduated and was now about to be sworn as a full-time Orange County Sheriff's Office deputy sheriff. That was an extremely proud day for me, and I felt a huge accomplishment. I worked so hard to get there and by basically self-educating myself without extensive formal education. My mom was present at my graduation, and as I was giving my speech, I looked into the crowd, and at her, and I swear I saw my dad sitting next to her. I think it was possible, and if not in my heart, I believed he was.

Now new adventures and more unusual things were about to unfold. I went to the uniformed patrol division and worked with some wonderful human beings. People that became a type of family. You knew that those people were there for you and had your back during dangerous situations, and that in return, you would be there for them, whatever the cost.

Now once again in patrol, I would start being in places at the right time and experiencing things that I just had no explanation for. Let me tell you about one of those occurrences.

I was answering a call in a high crime area of Zellwood, Florida. It was a sexual battery on a sixty-seven-year-old African American female. When I got to the scene, there were several neighborhood women already there cleaning up everything at the crime scene. They were washing the sheets and doing the victim's laundry, including her underwear. That was all evidence I might have been able to use from her attack. They weren't destroying the crime scene intentionally, they just didn't know any better. They thought that by doing what they were doing they would save the victim embarrassment. They even had her take a shower, ruining any hopes for a rape test kit to be done at the hospital.

I was not about to let this stop me from finding her attacker. The rape of the victim was violent. She told me that the man that raped her was an African American male, maybe in his early thirties. She said that he was very physical and held a knife to her throat. She also told me how he caused her a great deal of pain. I knew he had to be caught before he hurt someone else.

I walked her property and found a jalousie window that had been pried open. I took latent prints from the glass and submitted them for analysis. One week later, I learned that I got a hit (a perfect match). The hit was on an African American male in his early thirties that lived in the Zellwood area. He had an active warrant out for his arrest. The original charge was for a previous sexual battery of another woman.

I began looking for him in the neighborhoods in Zellwood and was able to locate him. I arrested him on the warrant and transported him to meet with an Orange County Sheriff's Office sex crimes investigator. After being questioned, the arrestee gave a full sworn confession as to him being the attacker of my victim.

As a result of my actions, I received a Letter of Commendation from the Orange County Sheriff's Office recognizing my performance. I was also awarded an administrative day off with pay for getting a positive match on the latent prints that I discovered at the scene of the crime. That was great and rewarding to have been recognized but not as rewarding as it was to get justice for the elderly victim of the sexual battery.

In my mind, was I becoming one of God's angels? Was I now a protector of the people developing the skills to fight a form of evil? This was again something I was unable to answer. Why was it that I responded to that call? Why was I on duty that day? Was I meant to be there?

I became a member of the Orange County Sheriff's Office's Emergency Response Team. One day, we were training at a facility in Orlando, Florida, when a call came out over the radio that a plane crash had just occurred in the Rosemont, Florida, area. It involved two airplanes that collided in midair. We immediately responded to the scene of the crash. What I witnessed on arrival was unimaginable.

The fire from the crash had been so intense that it melted the fairing and tires on a motorcycle that was inside a garage blocks away. This crash took place in a residential area where there were numerous privately owned homes. One of the planes involved was owned by a former business owner in Orlando, Florida, and the other was coming in from out of state. The out-of-state plane carried a family of three, and the Orlando plane was occupied by the pilot only.

I interviewed a couple of witnesses at the scene, and the first witness was all wet. I asked him how he got wet, and he didn't recall. I noticed that several credit cards and his wallet was floating in his pool. He didn't realize it, but as the planes approached, he automatically dove into his swimming pool prior to the crash.

When I spoke with the second witness, she told me that she was the owner of the mobile home that the Orlando plane literally cut in half upon impact. She said that she would have normally been home from work already and would have been inside the home at the time of the crash; however, she had stopped at the local grocery store to pick up some groceries. I believed God was looking out for her that day.

I was assigned to remain at the scene of the crash all night and guard the remains. This was another moment in my career that would stay with me for the rest of my life. I still see things from the scene that nobody should ever have had to see. I thought throughout the night that the people that I was guarding were gone forever. In an instant, their lives changed, and as a result, so did their surviving family members and friends. It was just such a tragic way to die. I definitely hugged my family members when I returned home. One of the hardest things about my job was not bringing it home, and I hope I speak for all of law enforcement.

It didn't stop there. Call after call and incident after incident, things would continue to happen. Another example was I was working off duty at a local spring (a park) where locals would go to swim. The springs had real shallow points, and there were signs posted NO DIVING. It never failed though, there would always be someone that ignored the signs. On one particular day, I was working the spring. Something told me to take the ATV (all-terrain vehicle) and go to what the park referred to as the third landing bridge. When I got there, I found a young male floating in the water. He dove off the bridge and broke his neck from hitting his head on the bottom of the spring. I removed some gear and jumped in to save him. He was still conscious and talking to me. He couldn't move his arms and said that he had no feeling in them. I got on my radio and called for rescue.

When the paramedics arrived, one got into the water with me. I didn't want to move the victim from the water until rescue got there because I didn't want to risk doing further damage to him. The paramedic took off his badge and stuck the victim in the chest area. The victim didn't feel anything. The victim said to me that he didn't want to die. I assured him that that was not going to happen. Rescue transported him to the hospital. I never knew what the victim's condition was until years later. I saw the victim in a commercial on television. It was an insurance commercial. The victim was in a wheelchair and paralyzed for life. Such a tragic accident that could have been prevented so easily. That would not be the last time that I encountered somebody getting seriously injured at the springs. I pulled individuals out with similar injuries numerous times.

Now let me talk about a call I responded to in Apopka, Florida. It was a call about an African American infant that was being reported as deceased. When I arrived at the location of the baby, I found several adult women in a frantic state, and I was unable to communicate with any of them. An elderly woman was bent over forward, rocking in a chair with her arms folded in front of her crying. I kept asking where the baby was. The older woman stood up abruptly and placed the deceased baby in my arms. What a tremendous shock that was to me! I laid the baby on the counter and began CPR. I could not get a pulse. I continued CPR until paramedics arrived. I am so sad to say that the baby did not survive. The sixteen-year-old mother had the baby in bed with her and rolled over on the child in the middle of the night, causing the baby to suffocate. A tragedy for the mom and all involved. I still have moments where I relive that horrible event. I can only rely on God's strength and guidance to see me through. There isn't anyone else that can understand what those types of occurrences do to a person. But you have to find the strength and move on. You see, in my line of work, you were not really supposed to show your emotions. You would take those emotions and release them in private. Sometimes, it was quite difficult.

As you are seeing so far, a policeman's job was not all about alleged abuse of suspects of a crime or cops and robbers. It was about dealing with people during the worst of moments.

I would like to share a funny story with you about a court appearance I had to make. Please believe me when I say that when I appeared in court, I was always very professional. However, I just couldn't resist the way I behaved during this particular day. You see, I had worked a series of home burglaries, and I got a call in the early morning hours one day about another burglary that just occurred. On my way to meet with my victim, I saw a suspicious car sitting in the dark in a field. I stopped to check it out, and I found two guys sleeping in the car. One was behind the steering wheel and the other was laying in the rear seat. I saw several pieces of lawn equipment in the car. I called for another unit and asked that deputy to go to my victim's house and get the victim and bring him to my location. I stayed with the two suspicious characters. When the victim arrived, he identified all the lawn equipment in the car as being his. I arrested the two suspects in the car and took them to jail.

The humorous thing was that they were taking me to trial, and my court appearance was about this case. Well, when I was on the witness stand, the defense attorney asked me a question. The question was where was his client positioned in the vehicle when I observed him. I told him that he was asleep behind the steering wheel. I really didn't know where the attorney was going with his questioning, so I continued to pay close attention, and so did the jury. Then the attorney asked me if I had ever fallen asleep sitting upright. I said if I was tired enough that I probably had. Members of the jury seemed to be hanging on to every word. The defense attorney then asked me if I had fallen asleep sitting up, which way would my head be leaning. I answered that I didn't know.

And then he said, "Why wouldn't you know?"

And I answered, "Because I would be asleep."

You could hear a pin drop in the courtroom, and then the entire jury broke out into laughter. The defense attorney said that he had no further questions. And I was not trying to be funny, I just couldn't resist, and I was being honest.

After saying that, I reminisce back to an interview that I attended in order to get a position in a specialized unit. One of the panel members during the interview asked me a question that really set me back. You see, I later learned that he (a lieutenant) was a psychology major and was using his expertise on me in an effort to wash me out of the interview process. Having no formal education in psychology, I had to pause and think carefully about what was being asked. The lieutenant asked me if I thought of myself as being a humanical or mechanical person? Wow, humanical or mechanical. Where was he going with that? I wanted that position very bad and was not going to be outsmarted. I knew that this was becoming personal to him, so I asked for a moment to give it some thought. Then the shock and fear left me, and very confidently, I answered, "A little bit of both."

Well, that answer really perked him up because now he felt a challenge. So, then he said, "Give me a percentage."

At that point, more strength began to enter my body, and where was it coming from? My confidence grew more, and my fears left. I said, "Sixty/forty."

He said, "Meaning what?"

I said, "Sixty percent humanical and forty percent mechanical."

Well, this guy was persistent in winning and was not going to stop. He then said, "Which means what?"

I couldn't believe how answers just continued to enter my mind without hesitation. I now know that God was there with me because the answers I was giving was not something that I learned. Or could they have been coming from my heart. I responded by saying that I was sixty percent humanical because I believed in treating people with respect regardless of who they were, that everyone deserved the benefit of doubt until proven guilty, and that you should never take away a person's dignity. I then said that I was forty percent mechanical because I believed that going by the book was not always the right way. I said that the book was merely a guideline and that people were human beings and not machines, also that every case or incident was unique in itself. Well, he finally stopped questioning and said very good. So, by remaining calm, strong, and confident, I got through that interview and got the position. So, please, don't ever give up. Be confident and always keep learning. We learn something new every time we start our day. If we would just pay attention and realize it.

Then there was the time I was on patrol during a very rainy evening. I was in rural Orange County in the Apopka, Florida, area driving when I saw a man walking in the heavy rain. I pulled over to offer him a ride. He was very grateful and took me up on my offer. Once the man got into the car, he began to cry. I asked him if everything was alright. He said to me that he was a man of God and that he knew my picking him up was not part of my obligations or duties as a police officer. I told him that I saw another human being in need and that I was glad to be able to help. That man's great appreciation meant more to me than you can imagine. And why was it that I was there that evening to encounter him? Was this another message sent to me? Why did he say he was a man of God? I don't have the answer.

Let me tell you now about another unusual call that I responded to in the Apopka, Florida, area. I was dispatched to an apartment complex where a young female had reported a burglary to her apartment. When I was responding, I was driving up in darkness with my lights off. As I got close, I saw a white male matching the description of the suspect that the female victim had given to the dispatcher riding a bicycle at a fast pace away from the complex. I stopped short, got out of my patrol car, and waited as he was trying to ride past me. I ordered him to stop, and he refused, so I physically removed him from the bicycle. I detained him in the back of my car until another deputy could get the female victim and bring her to my location.

When she got there, she positively identified the male in my back seat as being the one that had broken into her apartment. She said that her roommate (another female) wasn't home because she had spent the night at her boyfriend's. She said that she was in a sound sleep when she was awakened by the male suspect standing over her. She screamed, and the male suspect ran. She said then she called police. I took the male suspect to the sheriff's substation that was nearby to interview him before I would take him to jail. While I was interviewing him, a strap kept falling down on his shoulder that was under his T-shirt. He kept pushing it back, hoping that I wouldn't notice. I asked him what it was. He said nothing. I had him lift up his shirt and saw that he was wearing a bra under his shirt. I asked him who's it was, and he didn't answer.

When I got him to the jail corrections, personnel also found that he was wearing women's panties. I photographed the items and took the pictures to show the victim. She identified them as hers. So, the male suspect had broken into her apartment, got undressed, and then put on her undergarments. What would he have done had she not awakened and screamed? What would he had done to somebody else had I not gotten there when I did and capture him? Why did I get there at the exact right time? Was it mere coincidence? I don't have the answers to those questions either.

I struggled with finding the answers for years. Was it that you would think that it was just because I was a good cop? I still think that there was much more to it than that. And I would continue to explain why I thought that.

Incident after incident would continue to unfold, and I would often find myself involved in things that seemed very different and unusual in comparison to others.

I would next find myself being dispatched to a home in the Zellwood, Florida, area. That area was known for illegal narcotics sales. I met with a man that called the sheriff's office to report a theft of items from his residence. He reported the identity of the thief as being his drug-addicted son. We spoke for a while, and the man provided me with details as to what had happened prior to his calling.

He said that he was at his job, which was not far from his home, and he got a call from his adult son. His son was asking that he come home and give him a jump because his car wouldn't start. That happened at about 11:00 a.m. The man went home while taking a lunch break and jumped his son's car. The man said that he told his son he was going to go into the house to relieve himself, and his son told him not to do that and just go behind the shed. So, the man did. When he got back to work, he thought about it, and his son's behavior seemed very strange to him, so he returned home. When he went inside the house, he found that all his electronics were gone, including the microwave oven. He was very distraught and upset because he knew that his son had taken them. He told me that his son had a crack cocaine addiction and that he knew that he took the items to get the money for crack. He didn't know what to do and flat-out refused to bring charges against his son. I took all the information and told him that I would spend as much of my shift as I could trying to locate his son and the items. I also left him with a business card with my phone number.

At about 7:00 p.m., I got a call from the man, and he was asking me to return to his residence. He said that he had additional information. When I got to the home, he was there, and he had his representative from church there with him. The man relayed that he went into his checkbook and found several checks were missing. He said that he knew his son was the person responsible, and after his talking to his church representative, he was willing to go through with prosecution. The man wept over what he was about to do. I told him that it was the right thing and assured him that by doing nothing, his son would be heading for self-destruction. I now had the power to move forward and find his son to arrest him. I located him in a known drug area and placed him under arrest. The things that were said between myself, the man, and the man of God that was present in the man's home were very touching and meaningful. There was so much of God's presence in that room. The decision was made through God to do what had to be done to preserve a life. His only son's life. The following day, I was able to locate the items that had been stolen. They were at a local pawnshop. The man's son sold the items to feed his crack cocaine addiction.

Soon after this incident, I found myself in an intense situation involving a vehicle accident while I was driving my marked patrol car. I was responding to a call for help from another deputy that was facing a subject with a gun. I was driving with my blue lights and siren running what we referred to as code three. I was coming up on an intersection where cross traffic had a red flashing light, and I had a yellow flashing light. I slowed somewhat and could actually see a male driver waiting at the intersection, then at the last minute, he decided to pull out. I couldn't believe what I was witnessing. I was heading straight for his driver's side door and knew that if I hit him there, I would seriously injure him or possibly kill him. I immediately took evasive action, momentarily hitting my brakes then steered hard right. I managed to hit him in the left rear bumper area and spin him around. Then I had to maintain control of my patrol car and steer between a telephone pole and a metal sign where may car came to rest just inside a chain-link fence.

There was smoke and debris everywhere. I couldn't get out of the car because the driver's door was so badly damaged. Rescue arrived, and they had to cut the door off to get me out. When they placed me on the stretcher to place me in the ambulance, I heard the other driver say to the Florida state trooper that was working the accident that he saw me and he heard my siren, but he thought he could beat me. This guy nearly cost me my life and jeopardized his own just because of his horrible decision-making. Believe me though, this was not uncommon in police work. The trooper at the scene said that I had done an amazing piece of driving. I owe that to my tractor-trailer experience and also my continuing collision avoidance training that we received at the sheriff's office.

After that, I began hitting the numbered streets in Apopka, Florida, pretty hard. The numbered streets were known for high volumes of illegal drug sales. That was due to an influx of Haitian immigrants in the area, and with them they brought and introduced Apopka to crack cocaine. Highland and 12th St. was the drive-through sales location, and it was nonstop. Business was very good until myself and other deputies came in to spoil it. We began making numerous arrests and began driving the crack cocaine dealers out of Apopka. We were hurting their sales so badly that an informant as well as command staff told us that the word was out that the Haitian crack dealers had taken pictures of deputies that they wanted eliminated. My name was one of them. But I felt that our gang was bigger than their gang, and we eventually hurt sales so bad that they left the area.

I am only one of many cops out there that have done the job or are still doing it. We are all human beings of different sexes, races, and ethnic backgrounds. We all care and try not to take the job home with us. It is a profession that you will never get rich in. Every time you leave the home, you never know if you will return. And I say this because I believe I speak for all cops. We serve the public or have served the public, and the vast majority of us are good. There will always be that few that ruin it, but that holds true in every profession. There are measures put into place to weed out the bad. Try and think for a moment. If there weren't any police in this country, in a dire situation, who would you call?

I am sorry, but I had to throw that out there so that you realize that I am not trying to take sole credit for doing a thankless job.

I started getting pretty good at running down and catching the bad guys during foot pursuits. My name began to spread throughout the agency as my productivity increased. I was very determined and persistent. I took an oath to serve and protect the public and took that oath very serious. As a result of my performance in the patrol division, I was awarded the Deputy Sheriff Frank Seton Award. It was an award that exemplified the characteristics and qualities of fallen Deputy Frank Seton. Deputy Seton lost his life in the line of duty.

Well, now after all the things that had occurred in the patrol division, I got approached by detectives from our criminal investigations division because they had heard about my background in trucking. They asked me to give going undercover a shot. They had a group working out of the Zellwood, Florida, area that had engaged in a chop shop operation. They were running a legitimate trucking company; however, they were also stealing trucks and disassembling them to use the parts on other trucks in their fleet.

I agreed and later found that the Federal Bureau of Investigation was also involved in the operation due to the criminal organization bringing those stolen trucks across state lines. I dressed the part and went to the property owned by the main guy in an attempt to sell him some stolen goods. It would be an effort to see if he was truly dirty and a way to secure a search warrant for the property. I had loaded up two Michelin semitruck tires mounted on two expensive

Alcoa aluminum wheels in the back of a pick-up truck. That set of wheels were worth approximately $2,000.00. They were donated to me by a local business owner. It was people like that in the community that made a huge impact by providing assistance to the police. Now think about this, I had never met any of these people. I had nobody to introduce me or vouch for me. I was going in cold and solely depending on my gift of gab. Which basically means how convincing would I be.

With a cover team in place including a member of the FBI being present, I drove to the property. I was wearing a wire so that my cover team could monitor me and record conversation between me and the bad guy.

I was able to make contact with the main guy involved in the criminal conspiracy. He was one of several family members that were running the chop shop and identified himself to me as the owner of the trucking company. My story to him was that I was an independent trucker (owner-operator) and that my transmission on my truck had gone out. My truck was at a truck stop in south Orlando down near Kissimmee, Florida, and I was in bad need of money. I said that I was doing anything and everything to get up enough money to get my truck back on the road. I told him that I had some expensive truck rims and tires and that they were hot. I said that I was trying to sell them at the truck stop but couldn't get anybody's interest. I told him that one guy I came into contact with told me about him and gave me directions to his property. I explained how awkward and uneasy I felt and was really not sure if I could trust him.

He asked me if he could take a look at the wheels. He told me to relax and that he was okay. After he looked at the wheels I had, he said that he was very interested and wanted to know what I was asking for them. I told him that I realized they were stolen, but I still had to get as much as I could for them. He offered me two hundred dollars. I said that the offer was low but that I was in a desperate situation and that I would take it. Then to top it off, he asked me if he could write me a check. Wow, what a break! This guy was actually going to write me a check for $200.00 drawn from his company account and write it in my name. It couldn't have worked out any better. What evidence!

So, I made the undercover deal and got my first exposure to undercover work. It provided enough evidence to help get the ball rolling in an ongoing FBI investigation. Through that deal, the FBI was able to get several search warrants to different properties owned by that criminal family. There was also information that members or a member of that family had committed a murder. I don't have knowledge as to whether or not that was ever confirmed.

When the FBI began serving the warrants, I was called upon once again. They knew that I had prior truck driving experience and they needed my help in moving twenty-six seized semitrucks and trailers to a storage lot on the east coast. Bruce, a sergeant that I worked with at the Orange County Sheriff's Office, also provided his services because he had previous trucking experience as well. We agreed and provided the assistance they asked for. When it was over, all the family members involved were arrested on federal charges. Numerous trucks, trailers, and other expensive pieces of equipment were seized and sold at public auction.

As a result of my expertise, dedication to duty, and contributing to the success of this case, the FBI awarded me with a Letter of Commendation.

I decided to take a little weekend break and go visit family in the Gulf Coast area in Florida. I was at the beach with my sister, her mother-in-law, and other family members. I looked out into the water and saw a few people struggling with an undertow, and they appeared to be drowning. Without thinking, I dove in and swam out to them. I saw a young girl, maybe eight years of age, going under, and I could no longer see her. I swam to where I thought she would be, and I reached below the surface and got ahold of her hair. I pulled her up, and she wrapped her arms around my neck in a panic, gasping for air. It was very difficult to swim with her because she was so frantic, but I was able to get her to shore safely. Her family members were standing on the shoreline waiting for me. They must not have spoken English because I was unable to communicate with them, and they didn't thank me, they just smiled when I handed her to them.

So, now yet another strange occurrence in my life. It seemed that I was not able to go any place without something like this occurring. Was I meant to be there? Again, I can't answer that question.

So, back to work. Now I got my feet wet and kind of liked knowing about my unique ability to communicate with the bad guys. So, what would be next? Well, I would soon find out.

It was an election year, and we at the sheriff's office were getting a new sheriff. We would go in at the start of the new year and find out what our assignments would be.

The assignments were posted on a bulletin board in the substation briefing room. I looked and found my name. Next to my name was the word Narcotics! Narcotics, I was now assigned to the street drug narcotics unit in Sector-1 in Orange County, Florida. This was a big surprise to me. But the sheriff was the boss, and if that was his decision, I would abide by it. I had made my mind up to give it my all as I had done in every other position I had been in.

Our unit got together, a few of the agents I already knew, and some I didn't. However, I would learn that they would end up being some of the finest people I had ever had the pleasure to work with. We were tasked with going out and finding an off-site location to work out of away from the sheriff's facilities. This would be an undercover office.

I would like to share a funny story about something that had occurred when we went to look at one place for rent. There was an elderly gentleman present that was trying to rent the place. We each introduced ourselves, but the man kept calling me Brian. I would correct him, but it did no good. His last name was Jomackski or something like that. So, being the characters that my fellow agents were, after we left, they continued to call me Brian. My sergeant started calling me Jomack. So, lo and behold, my undercover name became Brian Jomack. And that name worked very well because I picked up quickly in learning the undercover role and became highly successful at it.

Well, we did find an office, and it wasn't the one the elderly man was renting. We hit the ground running. Crack cocaine still seemed to be the popular drug for sale on the streets. I believe the locals picked up on just how much money there was to be made from the Haitians that they had encountered before their leaving Apopka. I had a female partner who was new to narcotics as well. She was great! She and I were making numbers of undercover buys and really making a dent in the crack cocaine sales in Sector-1. I soon established the name as being the cold contact king. That was because I could strike up a conversation with merely anybody, and if they were involved in any kind of illegal drugs, or with any illegal drug dealers, I could make an undercover drug purchase from them.

During one cold contact, I met a man on the streets and asked if he knew any place that I could buy some drugs. Maybe I didn't use those words, but I think you understand. He kind of looked like Willie Nelson. He said that he did and asked me to drive him to a house in the Lockhart, Florida, area. I provided him with US currency that I had copied the serial numbers off and sent him into the house. Now be clear that he did not know that I was a cop. He made the purchase and came back out of the house and provided me with the drugs. He said that the people inside the house had just replenished their stash and had plenty of drugs. I asked him if I could get his number and make another purchase in a couple of hours. He agreed. I called him a couple of hours later and myself and another agent that was with me previously, went, and picked him up.

We drove him back to the same location that he had previously purchased illegal drugs from, and he made another purchase for me with serialized currency I had given him. When he came back out and gave me the drugs, this time I arrested him. He cooperated and told me the number of people in the house and the number of drugs. We transported him to jail and made sure that he would not have access to a phone for a while so that he couldn't tip off the dealer. I would now start on a search warrant that would give us access to the residence. I completed the warrant and found an on-call judge to get it signed. When I questioned the subject before booking him into jail, he never said anything about weapons in the house. That information could have changed what would later happen had he provided it.

After I got the search warrant signed, I made arrangements with the Orange County Sheriff's Office Swat Team to join us and make entry into the drug house. It was the sheriff's office policy to use SWAT during the execution of drug search warrants. Entry would occur shortly after midnight. When we went to enter after knocking and announcing that we were police, you could hear people scrambling inside the home. Once SWAT made entry, one subject was running towards the front door from a front bedroom with a .44 Magnum handgun. One SWAT team member had another subject on the floor in the foyer right near the front door. The subject with the .44 Magnum pointed the gun at the SWAT team member's head that had the subject down. A second SWAT team member fired his weapon, striking the man with the handgun, fatally wounding him. There was a large abundance of drugs and currency inside the residence. The serialized currency that I gave the person to buy drugs for me was comingled with other drug currency in the home. There were also numerous firearms in the residence. Now this had turned into not only a drug search warrant but a homicide. This turned into an all-night investigation and went well into the next day. But drugs are a victimless crime, right?

I soon got involved in another case where I got information about a major marijuana distributor in the Zellwood, Florida, area. I had no source of assistance, no informants, or any other way to get into that operation. So, I decided to put a cover team together, and I was going to just walk up to the front door of the location and strike up a conversation with the bad guy. When I knocked on the door, he answered, and it was very awkward.

I said to him, "Hey, man, I really feel uncomfortable 'cause I don't know you, but I was at a bar in Apopka that I hang out at, and I ran into a couple of guys that I got to drinking with. After a while, I asked one of them for some weed. He said he didn't have any, and he gave me your address and said that you could hook me up." I said that I felt really stupid and I wouldn't blame him if he slammed the door in my face.

He laughed and said, "You aren't the police, are you?" I laughed and said heck no! He grabbed my shirt and said, "Get in here."

He brought out a briefcase and opened it in front of me. It was full of one-ounce bags of marijuana that looked to total out to over one pound. He let me pick out the bag I wanted, and I gave him the serialized currency. I asked him if I would be able to return and make future buys, and he said yes.

Well, needless to say, I did return hours later with a team of drug agents and a search warrant in hand. I knocked on the front door, and a woman answered. She directed me to the barn at the rear of the property where she said I would find my bad guy. When we opened the side door to the barn, I saw my bad guy sitting at a desk with about twenty pounds of marijuana on top of the desk. He was removing the stems and bagging the marijuana into one-pound bags. When he saw me, he said, "Are you back so soon?"

I said, "Yes, and remember when you asked me if I was the police and I said no?"

He said, "Yes."

And I said, "I lied."

He literally urinated in his pants right in front of me. He went to jail, and we seized a large number of drugs. And it was all accomplished off a cold contact. And just for you sceptics, you are allowed to lie when in an undercover role.

Well, I started working out at a gym in Apopka, Florida. I got to know the owner and his longtime girlfriend. They didn't know what I did for a living, and I surely didn't volunteer that information. Well, as time passed and after several visits to the gym, I started noticing different things that appeared unusual to me. During one visit, I noticed the owner John blow up with anger. That behavior was consistent with steroid use. It was referred to as 'roid rage. Also, John was a very large man, and his muscular structure was not attained merely from working out.

Then one day, I was in the gym and an elderly woman came in and started shouting at John. She was yelling at him about his providing her grandson with steroids.

Visit after visit, something different would happen. I started noticing several members of the Warlocks motorcycle club frequenting the gym. Even the club's national president, Spike, Gunner, the club's enforcer (or Wayne), would also come in regularly. I knew Gunner (or Wayne) because I bought a new Harley Davidson from him when he worked at Seminole Harley Davidson. Wayne seemed to be a pretty good guy but soon met his fate. He was a family man with a daughter. My understanding was that his daughter had a new boyfriend that was leading her astray. Wayne didn't approve and forbid her from seeing him.

So, Wayne's daughter and boyfriend hid in Wayne's house and waited for him to come home. Wayne was attacked with a gun or guns and shot. By which of the two, I really don't know, maybe both. Wayne died from his injuries.

Well, now John's girlfriend began being open with me while I worked out and would complain about John's drug usage and anger flare-ups. She would tell me about John's illegal drug activity that involved the Warlocks motorcycle club members. I continued to work out at the gym and gather vital information about the criminal activity taking place. I held that information and continued to form a case until I could find the right person, or persons, with the experience and knowledge to work something at that level. I was never about making a name for myself. I was about protecting the public and bringing the bad guy to justice.

Next, I made contact with a trucking company in the Apopka, Florida, area and asked if they would loan me a semi-tractor for undercover use. The company owner agreed, and I got the truck. I set up an undercover operation for the Apopka, Florida, numbered streets. That was an area known for wide open illegal drug sales. Me and my drug squad would conduct the operation. I was the driver and undercover agent. My squad positioned themselves in the sleeper with a video camera. That night, we were able to make approximately forty drug arrests. The drug dealers never imagined a semitruck driver would be a cop.

One arrest that night was actually quite humorous. I drove up to an African American female and asked her if she knew where I could buy some crack. Not exactly in those words but by using street slang. She said she did, and she climbed up into the passenger side of the semi.

Now just so you know, this was a cab over truck with a sleeper that sits high off the ground. The other drug agents were in the sleeper with the curtain closed and filming. She introduced herself as Peaches. Both of her earlobes were infected due to a bad piercing job, and they were badly swollen with fluid. She told me that her boyfriend would bring the crack, and she instructed me to circle the block. While I was driving, she reached back and opened the curtain and saw the drug agents in the sleeper with a video camera.

She looked at me and said, "What are all of those police doing back there?"

I said, "Police, are you high on crack? I don't go in your purse, please don't be looking into my sleeper. You are starting to freak me out, you must be seeing things." And we laughed.

Believe it or not, she went ahead and had her boyfriend get into the passenger side with her, and he sold me the crack. When we went to make the arrest, he jumped out of the truck and took off running. I was able to get out quicker than the other agents, and I was able to run him down and catch him. When I did, we landed in a bed of fire ants. He got bitten, so I had to hose him down with water. When I put him in the sleeper, he was all wet, and he got the mattress wet. When I got him to the jail, I had the medical staff look at him so that they could treat his ant bites.

When I returned the truck to the company owner, I told him about our success and the number of arrests we made. I also told him about how grateful we were for the use of the truck and his contribution to the community. He was pleased about the outcome, and then he said he just had one question. He asked me who urinated in his sleeper. I laughed and told him that nobody did, and I explained what really happened. He thought that was funny.

That year, our unit was given an award from the Veterans of Foreign Wars (VFW) for making record illegal drug arrests and cleaning up the streets of Apopka.

I was adapting to this new role so well that I felt that it was time to step up things and find a way to go after the real problem. That in my mind was the big dealer. The source and not the street-level seller. I am trying to find the right name. Drug kingpin? Well, whatever, I'll just say the big man.

There was an opening posted for a narcotics agent in a multia-gency, multi-jurisdictional drug task force in Orlando, Florida. It was the Metropolitan Bureau of Investigation, (MBI). This was a mid to upper-level narcotics unit that also had a vice unit and a white-collar crimes unit. Wow, it sounded so intriguing and important. They worked mid to upper-level narcotics violators. That seemed like something that I really wanted as a new challenge, so I put in for the position.

I went to my interview, and I felt that it went well. I was right because they called me before I even got back to Apopka. I was offered the spot, and I accepted immediately. I would now become an MBI narcotics agent. It would now be the chance to go after the big man or big fish.

But to my surprise, I got a call from my undersheriff, and he asked me to meet with him in his office. Wow! What could that be all about? I met with him in his office, and he told me that my reporting to MBI would be delayed for a bit. He said that the Volusia County Sheriff's Office was having problems with in-house corruption and that they needed outside help. He said that Orange County Sheriff's administrative staff had discussions as to who would best be suited for the role and that they selected me. That was quite an honor, how-ever, very little detail about the assignment that was given to me.

The undersheriff gave me the name and number of a contact person that was employed with the Volusia County Sheriff's Office and told me to get with him. He also said that he didn't want any details about the case that I would be working. He only asked that I check in with him every couple of weeks to let him know I was ok.

Well, I accepted the assignment and made my contact. I met with the person at the Volusia County line near Deland, Florida. He told me where an off-site undercover office was set up and set a time for me to be there. He also provided me with an undercover vehicle and the use of a Harley Davidson. He provided me with undercover funds and the ability to purchase housing at a hotel of my choice. I selected the Hampton Inn near the Daytona Beach airport to start because the undercover office was located in the old control tower at the airport, so it would be close by.

A briefing was held at the tower, and everyone involved in working the case was present. That was when I learned the details. There was a Volusia County Sheriff's employee that was suspected of being associated with a Lebanese family in Volusia County, specifically the Daytona Beach area. He was the owner of an offshore fishing vessel. Members of the Volusia County Sheriff's Office felt that far too much money was going through the employee's hands and his salary didn't justify it.

The Lebanese family involved was suspected of importing illegal hash and exporting illegal firearms. The head of the organization's name was Sammy. He was also an owner of an offshore fishing vessel. He had a home in Daytona Beach.

I started out my assignment by working undercover in the Volusia County Sheriff's operations center. I was supposed to watch the activities of the Volusia employee. During my time spent at operations, I saw large sums of cash on the employee's desk and documented what I observed. While I was there, I was able to make contact with a Volusia County Deputy that worked undercover as a biker (a one percenter). He really looked the part, and he rode an old Harley Panhead. His name was Rob, and he told me about a partner of his named Steve that was employed with the ATF (Alcohol Tobacco and Firearms). I will talk about these two later on because they became key figures in the Apopka gym case that I was involved in. Could these be the two I was looking for regarding the Apopka gym?

Well, back to the Volusia County case. And I will talk about them later on.

I was now pulled from Volusia County operations and began helping with the surveillance on Sammy. We followed him daily and were desperately trying to put a tracking device on his vehicle. The Florida Department of Law Enforcement was heading the operation.

Sammy parked his vehicle in his garage every night, so it was impossible to affix the tracking device.

One afternoon, we were following Sammy, and he pulled into a drive-through at a bank in Daytona Beach. We were two cars behind him. I told the agents in the car that I was in, that I would put the device on Sammy's vehicle at that moment. They looked at me like I was crazy. The device was magnetic, so it would attach easily.

I got out of the car with the tracking device and walked past the car in front of us. There was a woman driving that car. I dropped down on the ground at the rear of Sammy's car and slapped on the tracker. I got up, looked at the woman driving the car behind Sammy's car, smiled at her, and put my finger up to my mouth as if to be saying shhhh! The woman smiled back and never said a word.

We now had the tracking device in place. Sometimes, drastic things require drastic measures. After installing the tracker, we pulled over into a field across from the bank. I got out to take a break, and I noticed a lot of California plates on vehicles nearby. I also noticed some guys playing football in the field. One of the players missed a pass, and the ball came towards me and bounced at my feet. I picked up the ball, and the player that missed the pass walked towards me. He put out his hands for me to throw the ball to him, so I did. He looked familiar to me, but I didn't pick up on who he was right away. Somebody shouted out, "Don't you know who that is? That is Tom Cruise." Tom Cruise lowered his orange iridium glasses and smiled at me.

Oh my gosh, it really was Tom Cruise! They were filming the movie *Days of Thunder*. Then I started picking up on things around me. I saw Robert Duval walking across the field with a blonde woman. I heard screeching tires coming from a nearby parking garage. They were filming the scene where Cole Trickle was speeding through the garage in a rental car, and they were using stunt drivers.

So, after that fun experience, we got back to work. It was time again to focus on Sammy. We continued to follow him, and I continued on with surveillance reports and documented anything suspicious. I moved around and stayed at different hotels in Daytona Beach. We worked on establishing Sammy's ties with the Volusia

County employee and also his link to the illegal drug and firearms trade. Eventually, my assignment came to an end, and I would finally return to Orange County to start my new position in MBI. FDLE continued with the case, and I never really learned the end result.

Well, I finally got my start in MBI, and it would now become a whole new ball game. The Sammy case helped me somewhat because I was getting even more acclimated with larger-scale cases. But now in MBI, I would have to start at a certain level of purchase unlike working street drugs. You had to be able to convince a drug dealer to sell you a trafficking number of drugs during the very first buy. That was not an easy task. That meant that if you were buying cocaine for example, you would have to get the seller to provide you with at least 28 grams during the very first purchase. I thought that it was unreasonable and brought my concerns to the command staff's attention. I explained that it would be more reasonable to be able to gain the trust of the dealer by making smaller purchases then work your way up to the larger scale buys. They did not want to listen to reason, so I explained that maybe it would be better for me to go back to my old unit where I could be an effective narcotics agent.

That may have changed their minds, I don't know, but I am glad they did because I would go on to be one of the most effective MBI narcotics agents in MBI history. And MBI was one of the oldest task forces in the history of the US. It had been established in 1978.

So, I went back to my old ways from the street drug unit by making cold contacts and buying drugs, even street-level amounts. I would work those cases up to trafficking amounts and was making trafficking arrests left and right. In a trafficking case, if the sale of cocaine was more than 28 grams, the sentence was a minimum mandatory three years in prison for the defendant. If the sale was more than 400 grams, the sentencing was a minimum mandatory fifteen years in prison. I was really catching on and felt that I was making a difference in the community just as I had hoped to.

Now it was time to step up my game and go after drug organizations.

My MBI partner, Larry, and I were approached by MBI command staff and asked to look at a case that the Orlando Police

Department was working. We met with Orlando Police Officers and was provided with a great deal of reports that involved a crack cocaine organization that was working out of their city.

That group was moving large quantities of crack throughout the central Florida area and elsewhere. The Orlando Police had gone as far as they could with the case and was now turning everything over to me and Larry. Larry and I started doing some digging of our own. We pulled property records, vehicle records, identified family members, and other coconspirators involved in the criminal organization. We pulled criminal histories on the persons involved and learned that the majority of them had a history of drug trafficking. This was really turning into something big.

Now we had to figure a way to get to the heart of things. A wiretap? Yes, a wiretap would be the answer. But first, we would have to establish what was called probable cause. Probable cause was what any prudent and reasonable person would believe to have happened or reasonable grounds to believe. How would we get that? First, we would start obtaining phone records by issuing subpoenas to various phone companies (cellular and hard lines). These records would pertain to members of the organization's telephones. Then we would run the subscriber information regarding the names on the phones and the names that the members were calling to search criminal histories. We were getting a lot of previous drug arrest histories on people that members of the crack organization were calling. Now what would be next? A pen register? Yes, a pen register. To get a pen register, you would only need reasonable suspicion that criminal activity was occurring within the group. Which means I could establish reasonable suspicion through my training and experience as a law enforcement officer.

So, we got started writing. It was not an easy task. So much paperwork, so much time passing, and so many drugs being peddled on the streets of Orlando. But laws were laws, and if we didn't abide by them, we were no better than the criminals. And my name and reputation meant everything to me.

So, after a number of weeks of surveillance, and also endless phone research, we had enough to write the pen. Then after completion, it would go back and forth to our MBI legal staff. Was this what I had signed up for? Did I really know about all the time and lengthy documentation that was involved in all this? This was nothing like street drugs. Yes, in street drugs, you had reports to complete but nothing near as lengthy or complex as this. And you better have all your eyes dotted and your tees crossed before it goes to the judge. I was used to writing search warrants and arrest warrants, but they were nothing like this.

Larry and I began watching a house located on the west side of Orlando. That was a place that Orlando police agents provided us information about that they said was the home of the main target in the crack cocaine organization. That suspected target was also the owner of a well-known barbecue restaurant in the city of Orlando, Florida. We sat and watched day in and day out at all different times of day and never observed any activity at the residence. We didn't even see a vehicle at the location.

Orlando agents also provided us with documentation for vehicles registered to their suspected main target. One was a Datsun 240Z. We also went to the barbecue restaurant numerous times and never observed the 240Z there. Well, we now gathered enough evidence to establish enough probable cause to turn this into a full-blown wiretap investigation. So, after even far more paperwork, we had enough to take it to a judge, get it signed, and flip the switch.

Well, we finally got it approved and went to the judge. We got it signed, and now there was the matter of our technical equipment agents getting involved. They were the guys that would get the equipment up and running so that we could obtain the evidentiary information. And what a great group of guys they were. They were very knowledgeable and always willing to jump in and help. We could never have succeeded in cases like these without them. And to be clear, any case I was ever a part of was never successful because of any one person. It was always a team effort.

Once the wiretap was activated (we called it flipping the switch), we set up our monitoring schedule and off-site location to do the monitoring from. We put surveillance team schedules in place, and we were pretty much ready to go.

We were up and running, monitoring phones and conducting days on end of physical surveillance. And the nightmare of paperwork had just begun. You had incident reports, judge's reports, surveillance reports. I think we even had to do a report to go to the restroom! Just kidding.

Through the wiretap, we were able to learn the location of the main drug-ordering house, a delivery house, an apartment being leased by one of the drug coconspirators, and another house across from the drug ordering house that the main target would monitor the illegal activity from.

We learned that the operation was being run very similar to an illegal drug operation being done in the movie *New Jack City*. You see, a person could drive to the drug-ordering house, place their order, and pay for it in advance. They could order crack cocaine or powder cocaine, then they would be instructed to drive to specific location and wait.

The illegal drug-ordering house would place a call to the delivery house and tell the drivers what to deliver and where to deliver it to. There were two different delivery drivers, and they both carried cellular phones. Their location was far enough away so that the money and drugs were never brought together. Yet the house was centrally located, so it was easy to make the deliveries from. They would switch cars often so as to be inconspicuous. Pops, who was the father and coconspirator of family members involved in the drug organization, had a house right down the street from the drug-ordering house. He was in charge, and he would sit on the porch and oversee activities occurring as purchasers would arrive and place their order.

They would talk in code over the phone in case they were being monitored by police. We had to figure out a way to break that code, and we did. We decided to listen to a couple of orders over the phone and follow one of the delivery cars. We watched the deliveries then stopped two different customers consistent with two phone calls. Just to give you an example of the code, "one four hard at the WD Gore green Caddy" meant one quarter ounce of crack at the Winn Dixie supermarket on Gore street and deliver to a green Cadillac. The customer would be instructed to have their passenger window down. The delivery driver would just drive past and throw the cocaine into the customer's window like a newspaper delivery person. We were able to get still pictures of that activity and also video footage. It turned out to become valuable evidence. If they said in code "one four soft," that meant one quarter ounce of powder cocaine.

This was quite an organization. They were moving far more illegal drugs than anticipated and making a great deal of money. The wiretap was critical. As a result of it, we were getting information we would have never obtained without it. We kept adding more and more coconspirators. We identified more vehicles and properties belonging to the members of the group. We would stop drug purchaser's vehicles that were consistent with calls, identify them, seize the drugs, and then arrest them after the operation was shut down. So, you see, police don't go out and kidnap people like they have been accused of for no reason. Yes, what is needed? Probable cause.

On one occasion, while I was acting as supervisor in the wire room, I remember one call that came across the wire that I found quite humorous. While we were monitoring the call, you could hear hammering in the background. The person on the line was from the drug-ordering house, and he was talking to Pops. The caller was one of Pops son's and coconspirator in the case. He was complaining to Pops about Pops youngest biological son (his brother) they called Pee Wee. You see, according to the caller, Pee Wee was using the product they were selling (specifically crack cocaine). And according to the caller, the previous night, Pee Wee got skeeted up and was peeping and freaking. He broke out all the windows in the ordering house, and occupants at the house were boarding up the windows. We took it that Pee Wee obviously had gotten out of control due to being so high on crack. That was why we were hearing all the hammering. Needless to say, Pops was quite upset with Pee Wee, but it seemed that Pee Wee continued to be a problematic child throughout this investigation.

During another call later in the case, the main target everyone referred to as Pops was on the phone. He was talking to an African American female we believed to be his wife. The call was from the

Miami, Florida, area. That was an area that a great deal of cocaine was coming up from into Orlando. The call went like this, Pops said, "I need one grand, do you hear me, one grand." The female agreed and acknowledged that she understood what Pops said. Pops said that he would personally drive down to get it.

We put a surveillance team together and actually followed Pops all the way to Miami, Florida, from Orlando, Florida. It's roughly about 240 miles. Pops was driving his 240Z. When we got to the area of Miami, we reached out to the local police department, and they helped us by sitting at the residence that Pops was going to. We had pulled records from the phone conversation and knew the address in advance.

When Pops arrived at the home, the assisting officer witnessed him meet with an African American female in the front yard and saw her hand him a package. We believed when Pops was talking to the female during the phone conversation and he asked for one grand that he was using code for cocaine. We thought that he would be picking up one kilogram of cocaine because a kilogram is 1000 grams (one grand).

Well, we began our surveillance back to Orlando, Florida, following Pops. And I forgot to tell you that we had brought the Drug Enforcement Administration into this case once we flipped the switch on the wiretap. They adopted the case due to the large amounts of crack cocaine being distributed by the organization and also due to it being now labeled as a continuing criminal enterprise which if convicted of, you could face life in prison. That was also how we expanded our jurisdiction. DEA along with the United States Attorney's Office put an enormous amount of effort in this case and added to its success.

When we got into the Orlando city limits coming back from Miami on the Florida Turnpike, we decided to have an Orlando police marked unit conduct a traffic stop on Pops. Once we got him stopped, we had a drug canine on scene that checked for the presence of narcotics. The dog kept focusing on Pops front pants pocket, indicating that he had drugs. None were found by the officer. Pops told him that he had a small amount of weed and he threw it out when he was being pulled over. We did find one grand in Pops's possession (one thousand dollars), which at the time didn't make sense but later on in the case did. I will explain later.

Well, Pops was released for the time being, and the entire incident was documented.

We were getting to the point where we had enough evidence on all the members of the organization. We had identified properties owned by them, we identified coconspirators, we identified vehicles, and now it was time to start making arrests and take down the whole organization. We kept the wiretap running so as to get additional evidence once we started apprehending all parties involved. Because people love to talk.

Larry and I began putting lis pendens on all the real properties owned by Pops. Lis pendens is a formal notice that a lawsuit is pending and stops someone from selling the property involved. Lis pendens is a Latin term for suit pending.

Well, we rounded up all the persons we had charges on except one. Yes, we were still looking for, believe it or not, of all persons, Pee Wee. And now I will share another funny incident that occurred. We began seizing vehicles used in the commission of felonies. As we were seizing Pops's 240Z, an African American male pushed through the crowd and said, "You can't take that car, that's my Pops's car!"

We said, "And who are you?"

He said, "I am Pee Wee."

Well, I think you know what happened at that moment. Yes, we still took the car, and, yes, we took Pee Wee.

We then began conducting search warrants and at an apartment being rented by one of the main targets (another one of Pops's sons). We found more than one hundred seventy thousand dollars in a bag in the refrigerator. I called it cold cash.

Sorry, you have to keep some kind of sense of humor in this line of work or it will get the best of you. There wasn't any other furniture in the apartment. We believed that the apartment was being used for the money to be temporarily stored that was generated by their cocaine sales. This was probably one week's profits. We think that it was counted and then moved elsewhere. These guys were not foolish. They knew to never let the money and drugs come together.

And remember, I said I would talk about the grand that Pops had on him when we stopped him. We believe that the main cash from the organization was being placed in banks by Pops's wife in Miami, Florida. That was why Pops drove there to pick up one grand. They had an arrangement that whenever he needed money, she would have it for him. And he didn't want to do what is referred to as leaving a paper trail. So, that was why he physically went to get it himself. We were never able to locate all the money generated from the cocaine sales by this group.

Now was time to get on with even more reports and documentation to prepare for trial because we knew there would be one. We had twelve people in jail on federal charges and numerous others on state and local charges. One afternoon, I was sitting at my desk working on reports, and I received a phone call. The caller was well-known defense attorney, Cheney Mason. Cheney Mason was one of the attorneys that defended Casey Anthony, the woman accused of murdering her child in Ocoee, Florida, and was found not guilty.

Mr. Mason said that I needed to come to his office right away because we put lis pendens on his client's properties and that his client was sitting right in front of him. Well, I knew that couldn't be true because Pops's was in jail, so I went to Cheney Mason's office.

When I got there, he had an African American male sitting in his office, and Mr. Mason introduced him as having the same name as Pops. This person had the same physical features as Pops, was the same age as Pops, and did have the same legal name as Pops. His wife's name was nearly the same as Pops's wife, and he drove a 240Z. He even owned property on the same street that Pops would stay at to observe activity at the drug-ordering house.

I now realized that when the Orlando Police Department started their investigation, they linked these two men together through mere coincidence. They documented the person's properties belonging to the wrong Pops that owned the barbecue restaurant in Orlando and linked them to Pops the cocaine dealer. Larry and I took the information and ran with it. We never found anything to indicate that their information was not accurate. We would not have taken it at face value had there been any clues indicating something wasn't right.

Well, there was no damage done, I just lifted the lis pendens on the barbecue restaurant, and left them in place on cocaine dealer Pops's properties. I also pointed out to Cheney Mason that I would not have been suspicious of his client for wrongdoings had he not had four social security numbers. I also found that he owed the IRS a significant amount of money under one of them.

Well, Mr. Mason told me after learning that his client was not upset and that he may even name a barbecue sandwich after me. I was later quoted by the newspaper as saying that all this was like something out of *The Twilight Zone*.

Then trial preparations began. The family members that were the main source responsible for running this organization, after consulting with their attorneys, decided to take the case to trial.

The first task given to me by the United States Attorney's Office, assistant US attorney assigned to the case, was to extract and transcribe 300 calls from wiretap tapes that would be used as evidence in court. That took me approximately two weeks of just sitting at a desk with headphones on listening to certain calls and transcribing. During that time, a whole lot of excitement went out of police work. But your case didn't just start and end during arrests. You have to have a solid case to get convictions. And we knew that the group had the money to hire high-dollar attorneys that would use every tactic that they could to get their clients off. We were not going to let that happen.

Well, the trial began, and I was the government's key witness. That meant that I would be in the courtroom the entire time, and I was able to here all the testimonies from all parties involved. When it was time for me to get on the witness stand, I thought my time up there would never end. I was badgered by multiple defense attorneys over and over. When you experience things like that, you start asking yourself, is all this worth it? Is this what I really signed on for? Well, I found the answer to be "Yes, it was worth it." I took an oath to serve the people of this country, and I was going to do it to the best of my ability. And no matter what kind of pressure was put on me, I was going to be truthful and not going to crumble. One of the most interesting things to me in that courtroom during the trial was the moment we played the first evidence call for all to hear. You could hear a pin drop in the courtroom. You see, they never realized just how much damning evidence we had.

There was one point during trial preparations that we were able to do a proffer on the youngest defendant. A proffer is when you allow a defendant to cooperate, and if he or she is truthful and forthcoming about the case and what their involvement was, you can offer them a deal or lighter sentence. Well, during the proffer, the defendant refused the offer and said that blood was thicker than water and he was going to take his chances. I tried to tell him that he was a stepson so he didn't have the same blood and that he was looking at a possible lengthy sentence in prison if he was convicted. He didn't want to hear it. I was actually feeling sorry for him because he was only nineteen years old. And I didn't usually feel sorry for persons that intentionally continued to make bad decisions.

Well, there ended up being twelve defendants that were convicted on federal charges when the trial was over. There were also numerous defendants convicted on state and local charges in this case. And after I tell you the sentences, the shame of all of it was that they all had opportunities to cooperate and they didn't.

In the courtroom, the day of the sentencing, I was unsure as to what the judge would do and what sentences would be passed down to the defendants. I had charged them with numerous drug charges, trafficking in crack cocaine (over fifty grams), conspiracy to traffic in crack cocaine, and running a continual criminal enterprise. It only takes two individuals to charge conspiracy and five to charge running a continual criminal enterprise. The convictions on these charges carried life sentences.

I remember him allowing the first defendant (Pops) to speak, and Pops gave no response. Then I heard the judge say, "I sentence you to be incarcerated in a federal institution for the rest of your natural life." There were screams from friends, and family members that were present in the courtroom, and they had to be escorted out.

The next defendant (Pops's oldest son) was allowed to speak. He said to the judge, "I have nothing to say, it wouldn't do any good anyway."

Then the judge said, "I sentence you to be incarcerated for the rest of your natural life."

I had a chill come over me. This was very unsettling even though I felt justice was being served. Then the third defendant, again he was sentenced to be incarcerated for the rest of his natural life. That was another one of Pops's sons. Then the next defendant yet another son sentenced to thirty years. And then after seven more lengthy sentences were given, it was time for the youngest, Pops's stepson.

During the trial, a final effort was made by one of the assistant US attorneys on the case for the government to plead with the stepson's attorney. He leaned over to the stepson's defense attorney and asked that he reconsider the government's previous offer during the proffer. The defense attorney became irate and got into the assistant

US attorney's face and became very aggressive towards him. I was forced to step between them to stop his aggression, and then he put out his hands and said to me, "Go on, hit me, you would like to hit me in the face, wouldn't you?"

In all honesty, as much as I would have liked to, I didn't, I believe his behavior was planned in the hopes of him creating a mistrial. I responded to him as professionally as I could and said, "Sir, in all my years in police work, I have never witnessed such disgusting behavior. You are in a federal court of law, and you should act professionally and respect this courtroom."

I also told him that he was very close to being charged for assault and that he would look pretty silly being arrested in a federal court of law. The assistant US attorney turned to walk away from him, and he called the assistant US attorney a few choice words that are not suitable for this book.

The defense attorney finally left. The assistant US attorney asked that I write a memo as to what had happened that day and I did. As a result of his actions, the defense attorney was banned from practicing law in federal court for one year. That took a bit of money out of his pocket.

Several years later, I was going in for a deposition, and he was the defense attorney on the case, and he was giving the deposition. I remember hearing him say, "Would you please send in the infamous Rodney LeMond?"

I found that quite humorous. He was going to refer to me as being known for having a bad quality or doing a bad deed after the way he behaved in that courtroom. That was a clear form of hypocrisy if I had ever witnessed one. By the way, he acted very meek towards me during and after the deposition. Some lessons are hard learned, especially when it comes to someone losing money.

Now after having said all that, let's get back to Pops's stepson's sentencing. The judge gave him twelve years in federal prison. Wow, he would be thirty-one years old when he was released. And all, that could have been prevented if his attorney had any sense. Now he suffered as a result of his defense attorney's decision-making on his behalf.

For all my hard work, determination, and relentless efforts in this case, the United States Attorney's Office awarded me with a Letter of Commendation. I had to ask myself if this was truly a victory. A number of people going to prison for the rest of their lives and some going to prison for a better part of their lives. You may think that it wasn't. I think that they each had choices. The choice they made was to sell illegal drugs on the streets of Orlando, Florida, just for their own self gain and not even have consideration for what it might be doing to the purchasers. They didn't think of the lives they were affecting or the lives that could be lost while doing the drugs they sold. They didn't respect or consider the laws that were put into place to try and stop this type of behavior. They didn't show any respect towards the United States Attorney's Office when the deal was offered for their cooperation. So, yes, in some respects, this was a victory. The dangers they presented were eliminated from the streets of Orlando, and they would no longer be able to sell their poisonous drugs.

However, I had to ask myself, did the sentence fit the crime? Should a person who committed drug-related offenses be put in prison for the rest of his or her life when the courts were releasing known murderers in a much lesser amount of time. That was not for me to decide. That was way out of my decision-making authority. Let's say, it was up to the courts to decide.

The strict penalties and sentencing guidelines for crack cocaine sales and trafficking were put into place for a reason. At the time, crack cocaine took the country by storm and was being peddled on the streets in the US, like candy. If a person smoked crack cocaine, they would become addicted after their first high. It was a highly addictive drug and was being sold so widespread that extreme measures had to be taken to slow it down and hopefully stop it. When a person becomes addicted to a drug, such as crack, they will go to any length to get the money to purchase it. Which means rob, steal, or cheat an innocent victim out of their money or valuables and if necessary by violent force. The strict penalties seemed to have worked because crack cocaine and usage did taper off.

When this case ended, more things continued to happen. One day, Steve (an MBI sergeant) and I took a call from the Immigrations and Naturalization Services in Orlando, Florida. They were asking for help in locating a murder suspect. The charges were federal, and the suspect (a male subject) was charged with committing a murder on the high seas. We were able to do some research and find the location where he was hiding. We went there, made contact with him, and took him into custody. We both received Letters of Commendation from Immigrations Naturalization Service (INS), now known as Immigrations Customs Enforcement (ICE), for our assistance and efforts in taking a violent individual off the streets.

Now remember me saying earlier on that I would always try to do things in my off time to make extra money for my household? I started saving whatever I could and began buying repossessed big boats from a broker that I met. I would be able to put some money down, then I would finance the rest. The boat would be a minimum of 26 feet in length. They were in rough shape and in need of some tender, loving care, so that would allow me to get the boats at an excellent price. I would have them taken out of the water and placed in straps so I could start restoring them from the bottom up. One of the boats that I had done needed sanding and blue bottom paint. When I finished, I looked like a blue Smurf.

I was renting dock space for $115.00 per month that included water and electric so I could pull the boat around to the dock once it was back in the water and I could continue restoring it. We will call what I was doing gaining sweat equity. It was a great deal of work, but I was pretty good at it. I flipped a total of three boats over an approximate two-year period and did pretty well with my profit. I was able to take the money and put it into the purchase of a home with five acres of property. I also began putting money into the purchase of Corvettes over a period of time because Corvettes were always a popular car. I would put my skills to work by restoring them and flipping them for a profit. Then I found that Harley Davidsons became very popular, and I starting buying used ones in need of work. I would restore them and flip them for a profit.

Then new Harley Davidsons became very popular and difficult to get because demand was higher than availability. I made a connection with the owner of a local Harley Davidson dealership and was able to get my name on a list, and I started making purchases. I could buy one and then flip it for a profit, then put the money towards another new one. I did that until I had enough money to have one completely payed for. And I loved to ride my Harley Davidson.

I started a business hauling motorcycles due to them becoming such a popular past time. In the picture is the tractor-trailer that I had purchased and used to transport the items with. I also transported classic cars and eventually switched over to hauling travel-trailers and fifth wheels. It was fun being able to work and make the main motorcycle events. I was doing all this during my earned leave time, then when I retired from police work, went into it full time.

By my getting better known in MBI, I was developing numerous confidential informants. I received a call one morning from one of those informants, and he was providing me with information about a group in the Orlando area that was moving cocaine in large quantities from Orlando to a college town in North Carolina. The informant was deathly afraid of the members in the group, so he wouldn't get directly involved. He would only be willing to continue to provide me with information. He would finally confide in me and told me that members of the group were big steroid users and into martial arts. He said that they were trying to force him to let them utilize his legitimate business as a front for their cocaine sales. That was why he turned to me for help.

I came up with a plan to dismantle this organization. The direction I chose was to begin surveillance on locations provided, identify vehicles, obtain phone numbers listed to conspirators and coconspirators, identify all parties involved, and work on establishing enough information and evidence to stop their drug trade and send them to prison.

The end plan would be to flip that switch again. Yes, it was time to write another wiretap. That would take a tremendous amount of work again. Was I willing to take that on? You darn right I was. These guys were dangerous and threatening the streets of Orlando, Florida, as well as the streets of a city in North Carolina. I had to put a stop to it. And when I said I, I meant we. Even though I may have initiated the case, I wouldn't have been able to complete it without the help from my partner (Will) and the rest of the narcotics unit in MBI and again members from the Drug Enforcement Administration. So, all that work began all over again. The documentation, surveillance reports, pen register, and then wiretap. I think you got the picture.

I gave this case the operation name "Bonecrusher" due to information we received from the informant and other parties who had knowledge about the suspects' violent behavior.

We found out early on that the main suspect in the case lived near the University of Central Florida in Orlando. Well, that was of great interest to us because the town he was delivering cocaine to in North Carolina was also a college town. Was that his goal? Was it that he was delivering to and targeting college students as his customers? If so, we had to make a case on him as soon as possible and put a stop to it.

We started hitting places that he and his coconspirators frequented and began compiling information and evidence against them. My partner, Will, and I spent a great deal of time following them and documenting everything we observed. We, along with other members of the MBI narcotics unit, were able to compile enough evidence to turn this into yet another wiretap investigation.

So, here we go again. Long hours, piles of paperwork, multiple weeks or months of investigative tactics, and long periods away from home. Oh yeah, and did I emphasize how glamorous police work was? Well, I will say this, you only get out of it what you put in it. And that in itself was reward enough for me because you're definitely not in it for the low pay.

Well, now that we had enough for a wiretap, it was once again time to get with my contacts in DEA to see if they might have an interest in the case and see if it met their threshold. We would need them to again expand our jurisdiction. They showed a strong interest, and they came on board. Another joint venture was about to take place.

Oh yeah, something that I would like to point out. In order to get a raise or pay grade increase in DEA, you have to participate in a wiretap. So, we in MBI could do the vast majority of the work, initiate the case, provide the wire room, and then they could adopt the case or blue sheet it as they used to call it, and lo and behold, they would get credit. And also, at the state and local level where I was at, we could not get bonuses and they could.

And please don't take that wrong, I didn't mention that as a means of whining or complaining. I knew what I signed up for, and I knew what my salary would be. I brought it up because I wanted you to understand that the large majority of cops on the street work hard for the American people out of dedication to duty, to honestly serve the people, and do it with honor and integrity. It is not a get-rich job. The street cop faces danger every time he or she starts a shift. They face the unknowing. The unknowing if they are going to return home at the end of that shift. And they are doing it while most have to work at least two jobs to make ends meet. Another thing is that I am not going to ever say that there are not bad cops because I would be lying. But our job was and always should be to weed them out and see that they never put on a badge again.

The federal agents are better paid, yet they, too, face the dangers that present themselves in the line of duty. They just don't do it as frequent as the street cop that's out there protecting you while you sleep. I had a great deal of federal agents that I would call friends and had the utmost respect for. I would never disrespect them. I am just trying to be as honest as I can in educating the public as to what I believe and have witnessed firsthand.

Wow, did I get off on a tangent. So, back to the case. These guys we were looking at were pretty active and very abusive towards the weak. During surveillance, Will and I witnessed their violence on numerous occasions and often felt helpless because we couldn't react immediately out of fear of jeopardizing the long-term investigation.

Well, we were able to find that these guys had a safe house where they kept money and drugs as well as the main target, Michael, keeping a great deal at his apartment near the University of Central Florida.

We now had enough to, as we say, flip the switch, and we were up and running once again. Up on another wiretap. We were compiling evidence against these guys and identifying more and more coconspirators.

We were monitoring one call where it sounded like the person on the line ordered a significant amount of cocaine. We decided to have the van that he was driving stopped after his purchase. When we would do this, we would identify the person, seize the drugs, and let the person go. We would go out and arrest the person at the conclusion of the case. During this particular stop, it was quite humorous. We had a marked patrol car with a uniformed officer make the stop. When the officer turned on his overhead lights signaling the vehicle to stop, the driver tried to throw a lot of cocaine out the window. The cocaine blew back into the vehicle and was all over the driver's clothes and his face. He must not have realized it, but when the officer approached the driver, the driver said, "Is there a problem officer?" He wasn't the sharpest knife in the drawer. Oh yeah, he later went to prison.

Well, we continued working the case again, identifying coconspirators and seizing money and drugs, and now it was getting to be the time to bring everything to a close. We got a call that indicated that the main target (Michael) would be taking multiple kilograms of cocaine to Boone, North Carolina, to sell to college students. It was now the time to stop him. We set up surveillance on him utilizing DEA and MBI agents. We were also utilizing the Seminole County SWAT team. We had a plan in place to stop him at a set location. When we went to initiate the stop, evidently Michael had a plan to not be taken, and the pursuit was on. We chased him through three counties and watched as he threw two kilograms of cocaine out of his window. We had to end the pursuit because of his reckless driving and the threat he was causing towards the general public.

But Michael made the mistake of getting on the phone and calling his home. He instructed his live-in pregnant girlfriend to destroy all evidence in the house. We already had agents in place near the home. We immediately executed a search warrant on that home, seized evidence, and arrested his girlfriend. The location that Michael called from was that of his longtime friend and coconspirator's residence, Steve. We immediately went to Steve's house and captured Michael after he jumped through the rear window of the home. Steve was also arrested. Steve was a heavy steroid user and was an extremely muscular person. Months later, when I went to interview him in jail, I didn't recognize him. He must have lost forty pounds of muscle from being off steroids.

The government wanted to conduct a proffer with Michael and in return for his acceptance and honesty offer him a deal. Well, I knew Michael better than the government through observing his actions during all the surveillance we had done on him. So, my job was to convince them at the proffer of just how dangerous Michael really was. You see, during the proffer, Michael was real mild mannered and respectful towards everyone. He was really putting on a show.

My job was to trigger something in him, and I knew just how. I had to attack his ego. And I also knew that Michael was not being truthful. So, I explained to Michael how we followed him often and watched as him and his coconspirator friend, Steve, would use their size and muscle to abuse people. But I told him that I had one question. That question was that every time I would witness it happen, Steve was always the one to confront the person they were abusing.

I asked Michael if that was because he was afraid to and he needed Steve to do the dirty work. At that point, Michael went from mild mannered to enraged! He shouted that he wasn't afraid of anyone and that he didn't need Steve to do anything. He said that he would take care of his own problems and eliminate anyone he needed to. Well, that demonstration of his behavior in front of the assistant United States attorney that was present was all it took. All deals were off as they should have been.

We later met with another coconspirator in the case and conducted a proffer with him. His name was Cam. We offered him a deal for his cooperation and a means of him reducing his sentence. Cam said that he couldn't cooperate out of fear of retaliation from Michael, Steve, and others in the group. We told Cam we respected that and understood. We told him it was just an offer. The proffer ended, and I left the DEA office where it was being held. I was going through a fast-food drive-through to get some lunch, and I received a call from one of the DEA agents that was present during the proffer. He was calling to tell me that Cam had just committed suicide after leaving the proffer. Cam drove his car into a bridge at approximately 90 mph on Interstate-95 in Volusia County, Florida. A tragic ending to a young man's life. And for what? Again, something I will never understand.

We closed this case out with multiple convictions, multiple seizures of currency, vehicles, and property, and a whole lot of changed lives. And still had not made a dent in the drug trade in this country.

So, now in an effort to take some time away from the tragic events that kept occurring in my life and a means of making extra money, I decided to get back to refurbishing repossessed cabin cruiser boats in my off time. My first was a 32-foot Century with twin inboard/outboard engines. I was pretty good at restoring things and very mechanically inclined. It took me about ten months to get that boat where I wanted it, and in the process, I was able to enjoy it. After the conclusion of one wiretap I had written, I decided to take the boat up to a beautiful place in Florida called Silver Glen. It was right off Lake George that runs off the St. Johns River. I kept my boat on the St. Johns River so within three hours, I could be there.

A great deal of people in boats would congregate there on weekends, and I was going to spend the weekend there to relax and unwind. When you pull into Silver Glen, it is shallow and you have to just idle with you outdrives up until you get into the Glen. The water is crystal clear.

When I was idling in that day, I was passing a rented 45-foot houseboat. As I was passing by, there were two young males in the water that looked like they might have been in their late twenties. I looked down at the one male, and he looked extremely intoxicated. He was holding the other male's head above the water, and that male's face was blue. I asked the one male if his friend was alright, and he said, "I don't know, do you know CPR?" My other half who was then my wife was in the boat with me. I shut off my engines, left her with the boat, and I dove in to assist. I took control of the injured male who was not breathing, and I swam with him over to the swim platform of the houseboat that he dove off. I got him on the swim platform and started CPR on him. I yelled at members on the houseboat to get on the marine radio to the rental office and call 911. I told them to tell the rental office that I needed rescue units at my location immediately. I continued CPR and was having trouble getting air to the injured person's lungs because his neck was broken so badly. The temperature was in the high nineties outside, and I was getting very tired. But I was not going to quit. I continued to do breaths and chest compressions and could feel I was getting a pulse. I had to move him though because I was kneeling on diamond plate, and it was causing excruciating pain. Also, a female cousin of the injured party started yelling at me, and she said, "If you let him die, I will kill you." She was intoxicated as well.

I swam with the injured man to the shore and continued giving him breaths as I swam. When I got him on shore, there was a registered nurse present, and she assisted me in continuing CPR until rescue units finally arrived. They told me that they had a pulse, and they transported the subject to the nearest hospital.

We both were devastated over what had happened to that young man. And because of alcohol and diving into two feet of water from the top of the houseboat. I went to a spot in the Glen where we were going to spend the night. I set my anchors and sat back to think about what had just happened. As I was sitting there, one of the persons that was on the houseboat with the injured person was passing by in a small row boat to go fish. I asked him if he had heard about the condition of his friend. His response was very casual, and he said, "Oh yeah, he died." I could not believe how uncaring he was. It ruined my trip. I pulled up my anchors, and we left. I don't know how anyone could stay and continue drinking and carrying on after losing someone close to them.

When I returned to work on Monday, I called the Marion County rescue office that had responded to the scene, and they told me that the injured subject had a small circle on the top of his head caused from him diving into a rock on the bottom of the spring. He also said that his neck was broken and that his back was broken between the shoulder blades. He said that if he had lived, he would have been paralyzed from the neck down. His alcohol level was extremely high, and he dove into less than two feet of water.

There I was again. I just happened to be there at that time. Why me?

Then I was reaching my twenty-fifth wedding anniversary, and we planned a trip to Hawaii. We were going to take a Hawaiian cruise to visit all the islands. When we reached Maui, we decided to go snorkeling. I was out in the water, and I saw an elderly man floating face down. I turned him over and was shouting towards shore for help. He looked like he had suffered a heart attack. A lifeguard came out with a board, and together we got him on the board and swam to shore with him. I was giving breaths to the man on the way to shore. When we got the man in, we laid him on the beach, and the lifeguards took over. They had the man lying on his back, and I explained that he most likely had water in his lungs and that they should place him on his side. When they did that, a great deal of water began to expel from the man's mouth, and he began choking. That man survived. His wife thanked me several times and told me that they were on vacation from Massachusetts. And yet again, another unexplained incident occurring in my life.

So, now it was time to get back to work and focus on drug traffickers. I started digging again and got creative in targeting head shops in the Orlando, Florida, area. A head shop is a known location that is frequented by illicit drug users and illicit drug dealers. They are known to sell items that are used to induce or ingest illegal drugs. I found a Florida state statute that made it a felony to sell drug paraphernalia. This idea was new and had never been attempted before; however, having the confidence that I did, I knew that I could make a successful prosecutorial case.

I knew that in order to charge the owners of the shops with a criminal offense and to get the state attorney's office to prosecute the case, I would have to prove that the owner had knowledge that the items he was selling to customers would be used to smoke or use illicit drugs.

I decided to go into one of the shops in an undercover capacity and personally meet with the shop owner. I talked with the owner and through conversation was able to gain his trust. My entire conversation was recorded by agents outside acting as my cover team. Everything went well, in fact it went so well that the owner gave me access to a private room that only preferred customers were allowed access to. I was able to purchase a four-foot bong or water pipe from him. He even instructed me how to pack my marijuana in the bong or weed as he put it. He absolutely proved that he knew what I would be smoking in the pipe he sold me.

I completed the charging paperwork and submitted it to the state attorney's office. They charged the case, and I wrote a search warrant and executed it at the shop. I was able to seize everything in the shop, and the owner, as part of a plea bargain, had to forfeit ownership of all the items. The owner pled guilty, and the case was a complete success. There were nonbelievers early on in this case; however, I made believers out of them, even our legal staff. In fact, this became a new thing in MBI as a result of my hard work and efforts, and other agents began working the local head shops.

On to the next case. I was able to identify a known cocaine dealer by the name of Tommy through an informant that I had been working with. According to my informant, Tommy was moving large quantities of cocaine out of the Miami Beach, Florida, area, and the informant said that he could put me in touch with him. I began conversing with Tommy on the telephone and negotiated a half of kilogram cocaine deal with him. A half of kilogram of cocaine weighs out at over 500 grams. In Florida at that time, to be in possession of 400 grams of cocaine carried a minimum mandatory sentence in prison of fifteen years.

After getting to know more about Tommy through several phone conversations, I learned that he had a coconspirator by the name of Ed. I got Tommy and Ed to agree to drive to the Orlando, Florida, area with the cocaine and meet with me. However, while they were on their way, we continued to have phone conversations, and as drug dealers do, they kept wanting to change the way things would be done. We continued to talk, and I was able to get Tommy to tell me where he and Ed were at. I found that they were at a hotel on Highway 441 in south Orlando. Myself and assisting surveillance agents went to that location and sat and watched.

After a short period of time negotiating, I was to able convince Tommy to drive up to the Lake Fairview area in Orlando where there was a nightclub, and I was going to meet with him and Ed in the parking lot and complete the drug deal.

We sat and watched the hotel and saw Tommy and Ed leave their room. Tommy had a package in his right hand that looked like it would be the half of kilogram that I was going to buy from him. As him and Ed were getting into their car, I saw Tommy placed the package he had into a newspaper, and he put it on the driver's side. They drove off heading towards the nightclub that I was supposed to meet them at. While they were driving, I was on the phone with Tommy. He kept trying to change things, so I made the decision to have them stopped by an Orange County Sheriff's marked patrol car.

The deputy talked with Tommy briefly then came back to talk to me. He said that he could smell the acetone in the car, so he knew that there was cocaine in the vehicle. I guess he still didn't get the fact that I already knew that there was cocaine in the car and that I set this all up and that I just needed him for the stop. I had stopped a short distance behind the patrol car so that Tommy and Ed could not see me.

We got Tommy and Ed out of the car and put them in the rear seat of the patrol car. We let a drug canine run around the car, and it gave a positive indication for drugs being present. I reached into the driver's side of the car and retrieved a half of kilogram of cocaine. The cocaine was tested and returned positive results for in fact being cocaine. In the state of Florida at the time, being in possession of more than four hundred grams of cocaine carried a minimum mandatory sentence of fifteen years in prison. The cocaine they had in their possession weighed out at just over five hundred grams.

There was a recording device in the patrol car, and Tommy and Ed's conversation was recorded. They talked about some very incriminating things, and it really strengthened our case against them. I had Tommy and Ed transported to the Sheriff's Office Operation Center and sat down with them in an interview room. My partner, Will, sat in on the interview with me, and I began questioning them. They waived their right to having an attorney present while I talked to them. They were a little hesitant to talk at first; however, after I explained in detail what they were facing and how they could help themselves, they looked at each other and said, "I like this guy, let's do it."

The two began telling me about how they had been in the drug-smuggling business for about fifteen years. Tommy explained how he was living in Miami, Florida, and Ed was living in the Republic of Panama. Ed would send kilograms of cocaine to Tommy through the mail from Panama at extremely low prices, approximately ten to twelve thousand dollars per kilo. Tommy was moving it on the streets and getting about twenty-two to twenty-four thousand per kilo. Tommy said that they had connections with the Cali Colombia drug cartel and that they could work off their charges by bringing in a large shipment of cocaine for me.

This was getting to be almost unbelievable. You would hear a lot of stories in my line of work, and usually, someone will say anything to get out of the situation they are in. But in order to be good at this job, you have to be good at reading people. You have to always keep an open mind and be smarter than they are. After further conversation with them, they went on to say that they could get the cocaine if I could provide the transportation. Well, this was all getting beyond my jurisdictional boundaries, so I decided to call my contact at DEA, Steve, because this could possibly be turning into a federal case.

Steve came to my location, and we sat down and once again, interviewed Tommy and Ed so that Steve could hear for himself what they had to offer. They shared the same information with Steve that they had previously told me about. Steve was impressed, and together we decided to work with Tommy and Ed in an effort to make this happen.

I contacted the state attorney's office and explained what I wanted to do as far as working with Tommy and Ed. I asked that I be able to file the charges on Tommy and Ed and let them remain at large. I got the approval, and we got started right away.

We began working out of the DEA office (Orlando, Florida) by confirming a great deal of the intelligence provided to us by Tommy and Ed about their involvement with the Cali drug cartel. They had given us contact names of persons they would meet with and locations in Colombia that they would go to in order to purchase their cocaine and smuggle it into the United States. What they had been saying was now being proven and was not just some far-fetched story being fabricated by them in order for them to stay out of jail.

Together, we came up with a plan to negotiate with Cartel members by offering transportation of their cocaine into the United States for a fee. We would provide the transportation using a pleasure craft, a 39-foot boat, with persons on board appearing to be on a pleasure vacation/diving trip. We would take the cocaine on board in open waters outside the Republic of Panama.

We were asking for a transportation fee of 1.3 million dollars. The name I came up with for this case was Operation Poseidon Adventure.

The negotiations were going well; however, Ed was very nervous, and it became obvious that it was time to let Tommy take over. You see, Ed had been given the nick name "Shaky" by those that knew him.

Let me share a story about Ed. Ed lived in Panama for years, and that was how he made all his cocaine connections. Ed told me about one occasion where he was driving his Alfa Romeo sports car and he stopped at a traffic signal. He had the top down and was just enjoying the day. He said that a subject came up to the car and stuck a gun in his stomach. Ed, being the shaky, somewhat clueless guy that he was, said "I don't want to buy a gun" and the subject with the gun said, "I ain't selling one." Then Ed, coming to what senses he had, said "Oh, oh, you're robbing me" and he gave the guy his wallet. So, you see, Ed had the contacts, but he had to be monitored closely all the time.

So, recorded phone negotiations continued for weeks, and then the agreement was finally reached. Cartel members agreed to the transportation fee amount, and they would provide the cocaine to be brought into the country. However, they wanted to see the vessel that we would be using. So, now was the time to put a boat and a captain under contract. We found somebody from the east coast of Florida that agreed to captain his 39-foot Chris Craft and make the trip.

He would make a significant amount of money, but the risk he would take was extreme. Cartel members were violent people, and if they suspected for a moment that this was a DEA operation, he could be killed. Tommy and Ed would also be on board and putting their lives at risk, but they were doing so in order to stay out of jail. There would be a fourth member on board, and he was also a DEA informant.

This was really going to happen. This would be the largest drug case I was ever involved in. And to think, it all started with my half of kilogram of cocaine buy. I think now that I really proved my point to the leaders in MBI about starting small and working things up. I was just glad they had listened to me.

This was all taking place just after Pablo Escobar, the drug king-pin and head of the Medellin drug cartel, was killed by authorities. Escobar was very active in the early '70s up until the late '80s. He was worth an approximate thirty billion dollars. He was responsible for the murders of cops, lawyers, and judges. He was also responsible for having a commercial airliner shot down, killing hundreds of innocent people because he believed a prominent politician was onboard.

Escobar controlled 80 percent of the cocaine trade throughout the world. He was a very powerful man, the Colombian people often referred to him as Robin Hood. That was because he would give money, food, and housing to the poor in Colombia. He was so powerful that at one time he was convicted on a charge and built his own luxury prison to be incarcerated in. That was where he did his time. Escobar was killed by government authorities in 1993. That may have been the result that allowed the Cali Cartel to gain strength in the cocaine drug trade.

Well, back to the boat shipment Operation Poseidon.

The Cali Cartel sent a member to Florida, and we allowed him to view the vessel that we would be using to smuggle the drugs into the US from Colombia. He was very pleased with what he saw and went back to Colombia to report the news to other members of the cartel. The ball was now rolling, and things were springing into action.

Now we needed some kind of good faith shown by the cartel, so we requested money for state-of-the-art electronics to be installed on the boat. They obliged, and the money was received. Now the electronics were in place, and there was also a device that would be used to track the vessel during its voyage.

Bosses were asking for yet more good faith shown by the cartel. You see, bosses were tough to deal with at times and definitely made things difficult when working a high-profile case such as this. I guess they have people to answer to as well, so we just had to do what we had to do. I felt we were pushing the envelope, but the request was made for the cartel to pay us $25,000.00 in good faith money. They were hesitant but agreed.

My MBI partner, Will, and I went to Miami, Florida, to cover a Hispanic agent that would meet with a cartel member in an undercover capacity to take receipt of the money. Will and I were riding in a Greenwood edition Corvette convertible. This was a car that I had seized in a previous drug case. It was Will's agency's turn to get the next seized vehicle, and lucky them, this was the car. Will's sheriff was generous enough, knowing that it was my seizure and that Will was my partner to assign the car to Will so that I could enjoy it as well. So, we took possession of the $25,000.00 without a problem, and our bosses now had their good-faith money.

This was somewhat surprising to me at how smooth this all went. That was because one other time, I went to Miami working with DEA to cover a covert operation. That time, a DEA agent was supposed to go undercover in a case to meet with a bad guy and receive a payment that would incriminate the bad guy and give them enough to charge him. At the very last minute, the undercover agent changed his mind about going through with the undercover meeting, so they came to me. I knew nothing about the case and had to learn my undercover role quickly. I can't speak badly about the agent because this line of work is stressful and very frightening at times. It is just good that he realized his limitations and listened to his gut before it was too late. I had to learn everything about the person I was supposed to portray.

This guy I was going to meet with was not stupid, and I knew he would be doing all that he could to trip me up. To top it all off, I learned that the guy I was supposed to be was a part of an illegal drug operation and a member of this organization. He had been arrested, and he lost a large amount of the organization's cocaine as a result of his arrest, and now I had to play the part of that guy and regain the organization's faith. Thankfully, the member of the organization I was going to be meeting with had never met the guy that I was going to play the undercover role as.

The uneasy thing about all this was that I would need to convince this organization member that I was not a snitch and that I was not working with police to save my own skin. I would have to get him to take a payment from me so that it could be recorded and videotaped by a DEA cover team. This was really going to take the gift of gab on my part. What if this guy had been sent by the cartel to shut me up (kill me) so that I couldn't give up any information to the police? Well, that was the risk I would have to take. I knew of the dangers involved when I became an undercover agent. I was determined to make it happen.

DEA techs wired me up, and I headed to the meet. And please believe me when I say I was very uneasy and uncomfortable with the situation. I met the bad guy in a parking lot that was wide open and in broad daylight. I introduced myself, and we began talking. Just as I suspected, he began asking me a whole lot of questions in an effort to trip me up. I held my own and felt I was very convincing. However, there was a moment where he reached quickly behind his back near his waist area. I gave him a shove and said, "What do you think you are reaching for?" He replied, "My keys, I was going to go to my car to get a bag to put the money in so that you can keep your case." Wow, I was able to pull this off with such short notice and absolutely no time to prepare for it. Well, he took the money, and DEA got everything on video and audio. The bad guy was indicted with the rest of the organization, and I did my part in making this happen.

So, now you know why I was shocked to see how smoothly this meeting went with Cali Cartel members and a DEA agent. After what I had to previously experience.

Well, after satisfying the bosses, we were now getting more demands from the Cali Cartel members. They were wanting the CI (Tommy) to come to Colombia and stay until the deal was complete. Tommy agreed because he wanted to do what he could to make this thing happen. We flew him to Panama after setting the ground rules while he was there. He would have to go back and forth from Panama to Colombia. He would call me and report in daily, keeping me apprised as to what was going on. We also had a DEA special agent assigned to Panama that would be Tommy's contact agent.

Well, Tommy was doing everything he was supposed to be doing at first, and then the trouble began. The Colombian Cartel members were providing him with cocaine and plenty of alcohol. Tommy began calling me at irregular times (like 3:00 a.m.) and crying on the phone because the pressure was getting to him. I would coach him and try to get his head straight and assure him that he didn't want to be the cause of this deal going bad due to drug and alcohol consumption.

Then the request was made by DEA to get some more good-faith money from the cartel prior to sending the boat over. DEA wanted the cartel to provide Tommy with $150,000.00. I talked to Tommy prior to his getting the money and told him how important it was to secure the money and get it to his DEA contact agent in Panama. Tommy assured me that he would make it happen. He knew what was at stake if he didn't do what he was supposed to do, knowing that he was facing a fifteen-year minimum mandatory prison sentence.

Tommy collected the money from the cartel and reported to his contact DEA special agent, Richard Fekete, in Panama. Tommy called me the next day crying and highly agitated. He was saying that he didn't know who he could trust. He said that the cartel was treating him better than the DEA special agent in Panama. He said that he was counting the money with the DEA agent and that it totaled out to $150,000.00. He said that the agent looked at him and said, "I only counted $130,000.00."

Tommy said that he told the agent again, "No, there is $150,000.00."

He said that the agent then put his hand on his gun and said, "Did you hear me? There is only $130,000.00."

Tommy said to me, "You know I wouldn't do that, I wouldn't take money, this is my freedom we are talking about." Tommy said, "This agent is dirty."

I told him I would report this to the authorities in Orlando, and I did so. I told him to keep his wits about him and maintain the course. I was told by the people I reported to in Orlando that this was a CI that I was taking the word of over a seasoned veteran DEA agent. I said, "No, I am reporting what I was told as I should do." And I said that whatever they did with the information was on them. This would not be the end of allegations of wrongdoings by this agent out of Panama, and I would talk about it later on.

Let's get back to the boat shipment involving Tommy and Ed. We were getting close to being ready to send the boat and informants on its way to the Republic of Panama. We brought Tommy back to Florida and continued with the operation. I along with members of MBI and DEA held several more briefings, and additional phone conversations took place between cartel members and our confidential informants to be sure that everything was in place and it was now time to make the move. The boat was now on its way. DEA agents, myself, and Will met the vessel down in Port Everglade in Florida to stock the boat with groceries before it set off on its voyage. We also had what's called bladder tanks placed top side on the boat to give it more fuel range.

While we were down in the stateroom on the boat talking to the informants and mentally preparing them for the trip, United States Customs agents boarded the boat armed with AR-15s. It was pretty hair raising. You see, they were very alert in noticing the bladder tanks and picked up on the fact that this could be an illegal drug smuggling boat. They, however, did not check the boat by name. Had they done that, they would have found that it was a federally registered vessel involved in a covert operation. I don't blame them because they had to act quickly and did a great job. Everything worked out, and we all actually had a good laugh about it.

Well, the Chris Craft was now on its way out of Port Everglade and headed to Panama all loaded with groceries, dive gear, informants, and fuel. I felt quite confident, but I found myself with my fingers crossed a lot.

We stayed in touch by phone as often as we could, and Tommy checked in with me most every day or night. One intense moment occurred while they were cruising and out at sea. They began to get low on fuel, and we had to make arrangements for a 200-foot Naval vessel to come alongside them and refuel their boat. While refueling, the seas were very rough, and one of the informants went through one of the boat windows and into the ocean. Rescue personnel had to pull him from the water. They had to use duct tape to reseal the window. They later laughed about it, but I bet they weren't laughing when it happened.

Well, we finally got the call. They made it to a water inlet in Panama. They were awaiting contact to be made with Cali drug cartel members. They sat about a day or two, and late at night, they heard a little Jon boat approaching their vessel being operated by two Panamanian males. The little boat was heavily loaded with kilograms of cocaine. So heavily loaded that it capsized, and there were kilograms floating everywhere in the bay. They said that it was a real sight to see the little Panamanian males swimming around, desperately retrieving the kilos out of the water and putting them back in the Jon boat. The Panamanians probably knew that if they lost the cartel member's dope, they would be dead.

According to the informants, the boat was finally successfully loaded with the kilograms of cocaine, 500 to be exact. That amount equals more than 1000 pounds. DEA decided to have the boat change course, and instead of traveling back to Ft. Lauderdale, Florida, with the drugs, it would stop at Guantanamo Bay, Cuba. There, the drugs were transferred from the boat to a DEA aircraft and flown back to the Orlando Executive Airport.

We offloaded the drugs from the aircraft where they were transferred to DEA evidence.

When the boat arrived in Key West, Florida, with only the informants on board, I was flown by a DEA single engine plane out of Tampa, Florida, to Key West to bring the boat back into the country through US Customs.

We were given authorization to stay overnight; however, the DEA pilot wanted to get back home to family in Tampa. There was a very bad storm rolling in, and I didn't feel very comfortable with his decision. But he was the pilot, so myself and one of the informants got into the rear seat, and the pilot and another agent rode in the front. After takeoff, the weather got far worse, and I became extremely concerned. There was lightening, heavy rain, and strong winds.

Tommy (the informant sitting next to me) kept shouting and saying, "I almost died on that damn boat, now I am going to die in the back of this plane!"

I had to keep calming him down until we finally landed in Tampa. To be honest, I didn't think we were ever going to get there. I was pretty darned mad about the decision made to not spend the night in Key West.

Well, now the boat was back safely, the informants were back safely, and the drugs were in country safely. Now it was time to start negotiating with the Cali Cartel for payment regarding the transportation of their cocaine.

There was one more thing that we did learn though prior to starting negotiations. Cartel members kept saying that they threw in five special kilos, and we had to find out what they meant by that. Tests were conducted on the kilos of cocaine that we had in our possession, and we found that five of the kilos were not cocaine, they were kilos of heroin. About 75 percent pure heroin.

Well, imagine that, the Colombians were now trafficking heroin. That was not normal. The Colombians normally dealt with just cocaine. But why not, a kilo of cocaine would bring them possibly $25,000.00 on the street, but a kilo of heroin could bring in excess of $100,000.00. So, the US now had an additional influx of heroin coming from another country other than Mexico.

Setting all that aside, it was time to establish a game plan and get the cartel to start talking money. They owed us around 1.3 million dollars for bringing their cocaine into the United States. It was up to us to make that payment happen for the people of Central Florida.

We started by setting up a command center at the Twin Towers hotel on Major Blvd. in Orlando, Florida. The negotiating started, and cartel members began making demands of their own. They wanted us to turn over some of the cocaine and the five kilos of heroin prior to them paying any money. That was not going to happen. They sent a group down from New York with a truck and trailer and a couple of other members in cars. DEA started surveillance with vehicle and air surveillance following the cartel members around Orlando. I was in the command center at the Towers, and we were positioned on one of the upper floors. Surveillance units at times got a little anxious, and cartel members became aware of their presence.

At one point, one of the cartel vehicles pulled up alongside one of the DEA surveillance units, and one cartel member said "Hey, can you tell me how to get to Disney?" then he laughed and they drove off. We call that getting burned when you are in a covert role. That kind of blew what we had going at the time, and that cartel group packed it in and they went back to New York. These guys were sophisticated at what they did, and we needed to be better than them.

We now had to find a way to salvage this thing. DEA had been using one of their informants to talk to the cartel, and he was posing as being in control of the dope. The cartel kept trying to get him to turn over some of the drugs, and he kept refusing. This thing was slowly slipping through our fingers.

I suggested that we insert my confidential informant (Tommy) back into the mix and have him contact the cartel members and tell them that he ripped the dope from the previous informant being used and that he was now in control.

We all agreed, and that was what we did. Tommy talked to one of the members that seemed to be calling the shots by telephone. Tommy told him that he ripped the dope and was very scared about what might happen to him. The cartel member was very pleased about what Tommy had done, and we were back on with negotiations.

The cartel member asked Tommy where the dope was at, and Tommy told him that he had it at a storage facility. The member said that he would be sending a group up from Miami, Florida, to take possession of some of the dope for good faith and then payment would be made.

We set up a plan where we would wire a storage facility with video and audio taping capabilities, and we would agree to turn over 300 kilograms of cocaine only. The deal was made, and we got started on wiring the facility.

In the meantime, we sent an undercover agent to Miami with a cover team to take receipt of the money once we turned over the partial amount of dope.

Now when things began going well again, a DEA task force agent turned things around by going into the storage facility and tampering with the video; he said that he was trying to make final adjustments. What he did would cause us to lose all video temporarily. Thankfully, somebody caught it and made the corrections prior to the cartel members' arrival.

The cartel members showed up, and the vehicles they arrived with were quite interesting. They had a station wagon pulling a U-Haul trailer. When they pulled into the storage facility, they removed a false floor from the station wagon. They put 100 kilos of cocaine in the false flooring and then put the cover back on it. Then they put construction tools on top of it, such as saws, hammers, tool belts, etc.

Then they removed a false wall from the front of the U-Haul trailer and placed 200 kilos of cocaine inside the wall and placed the cover back over it. They even had stickers to put on the false wall just the same as U-Haul that said RETURN TRAILER CLEAN. Then they used an ammonia-based caulk to seal it so that it would throw off a dog's scent.

Well, they had everything loaded up, and they were ready to go. They pulled out, and we began surveillance with multiple vehicles and also air surveillance. We started negotiations in Miami after the call was made to cartel members in Miami that the group in Orlando had possession of the 300 kilos of cocaine. We were not going to let this cocaine get out of our sight. We followed the group in the station wagon to the area of 434 and state road 436 in Altamonte Springs, Florida, to the parking lot of a Home Depot. A question we all had was why were they headed in that direction. That was not the way back to Miami. Then an odd thing happened. A conversion van pulled in, and cartel members of the van met with the members of the station wagon. They all got out. One of the cartel members began to disconnect the U-Haul trailer from the station wagon, and he connected it to the conversion van. Their plan was to send the conversion van down the Florida Turnpike to Miami, and the station wagon was going to take I-95 south to Miami. That way, if one of the vehicles got stopped and the other made it down there, at least some of the dope would have gotten through. Well, we could no longer take that kind of risk since this change occurred. The decision was made to apprehend all the suspects and take them into custody. We could no longer risk losing any of that dope and put it into circulation, endangering the lives of the general public.

When we pulled up to make the apprehension, one of the suspects ran. Myself and a couple of other agents gave chase in a foot pursuit. We chased the guy into a pool hall. He had taken off his shirt because he was all sweaty. He thought that would eliminate drawing any attention to himself. Well, he was the only Colombian male in the place, and he was the only one all sweaty from running and with no shirt on. He went quietly, and we had all the bad guys in custody. And we had possession of all the cocaine. Now negotiations for the payment of 1.3 million dollars began to break down. There was a partial payment, not sure if we got it all, DEA never revealed that to me. But once the arrests were made, further negotiations ended.

So, all in all, as DEA said in a press conference, "We got the drugs, we got the bad guys, and we got their money." The case was a complete success.

We arrested five Colombian nationals, we seized 500 kilograms of cocaine, 5 kilograms of heroin, and we seized at least $200,000.00 in cash that I know of. DEA was working the cash seizures. To add to it, nobody got injured, and all the bad guys got lengthy prison sentences.

I received an award for my initiating the case, but in all honesty just the efforts, success, and outcome of the case was enough for me.

Well, now it was time to do my part in keeping my agreement with my confidential informants, Tommy and Ed. Because without those two, this case would have never happened. I went to the judge that would preside over their drug case where I was the arresting agent. The judge and I went behind closed doors in his chambers, and I explained the boat shipment of drugs that Tommy and Ed orchestrated and gave the judge quite a bit of detail regarding the actual events and the outcome. The judge was so impressed and astonished that he said all of it sounded like a movie and that Tommy and Ed went beyond what was expected and that they had definitely placed their lives in danger doing so. The judge agreed to give them time served and dismiss the charges against them.

Now this case was finally coming to a close, or maybe not.

My co-case agent from DEA (Steve) that helped orchestrate the boat shipment out of Colombia reached out to me with new information. He was putting together another shipment of drugs from out of Honduras. Because I brought him into the Colombian case, he wanted to return the favor by bringing me into this one.

Steve had an informant that was an unwitting informant that could apparently put this case together. An unwitting informant is a person that does not have knowledge that the person or persons he or she is working with are members of law enforcement. This informant had contacts in Honduras. The Honduran contacts expressed the need for assistance from the informant in helping them get their drugs into the United States.

Steve instructed me to go and get a passport because I would need one. I would most likely be traveling to Honduras. I got the passport and was prepared for the trip. Now the negotiations to bring in a shipment of cocaine from Honduras would begin.

The unwitting wanted us to send him over so that he could meet face-to-face with the people that he would be dealing with, so we did. We didn't want the unwitting to actually be in Honduras because we would lose all control of negotiations. We made an effort to keep him close to Honduras but not actually inside the country. By letting him enter the country, we would not only lose control of negotiations, but we lose the means of protecting the unwitting.

If you have ever worked in law enforcement and have ever worked with informants, you learn early on that they don't always do what they are told to do. In this case, that was exactly what happened. The unwitting started becoming so swayed by the drug dealers that he stopped listening to what we were instructing him to do. The dealers wanted him to come into the country, and we were telling him not to do that. We couldn't confide in the unwitting and tell him we were police or that would have blown the entire deal.

The unwitting told us that he trusted us and that he trusted the drug dealers as well. He told us that he was going over and he was going to make this thing happen, even if it was against our orders not to. He went, and just as we suspected, things really began to deteriorate. And not only did the unwitting fall for the story that the drug dealers were feeding him, they even convinced him to bring his wife and kids. This was all turning into a nightmare for us. We were now not only responsible for the safety and well-being of the unwitting, but we were now responsible for the safety and well-being of his wife and children.

Since the drug dealers felt that they had gotten the upper hand, they were becoming more and more demanding. They were taking extreme control over negotiations and were now starting with threats. They told us that if we didn't meet their demands, they would begin by killing the children, then the wife, and then they would start sending back body parts of the unwitting.

Things were becoming very intense. In my mind, this was something I would ever be able to live with. The knowledge that human beings, especially innocent children and an unknowing woman, would be murdered just over a damned drug shipment. That was not a risk I was willing to take. You see, these people did not just make threats, they would carry them out. I learned by working this case with DEA that the unwitting and his family were actually being held by Honduras's drug gorillas. Taking a human life doesn't have much meaning to them, and they show no remorse when they do it.

It was time now to abort this deal and get these innocent people back safely. We continued to attempt to negotiate and get their safe return. We were able to convince them to release the wife and children, and they did. We achieved a safe return home. But now they were still holding the unwitting and making more threats. They told us that if we didn't meet their demands, that they would start sending us body parts from the unwitting as they had threatened to do earlier on. We had to do everything in our power to prevent that from happening.

We decided to completely abort the deal and convince them that the US authorities were on to us and that this thing had to be placed on hold, not only for our protection but for theirs as well.

Now we would just have to wait. We heard nothing for about a week. It seemed like the longest week I had ever spent. But then out of nowhere, we received a call from the unwitting. He was out! They had let him go. We met with him, and this time we identified ourselves as law enforcement. We obtained facts from the unwitting to confirm all the things that had occurred. All and all, we came out of this thing ok. Not anyone was hurt. Even though the deal fell through, I knew with the abundance of drugs coming into this country, there would be future cases.

After things began to slow down a little bit. I received a phone call from an informant that I had previously arrested in a drug case. The informant told me that he could make a multiple kilogram cocaine purchase from a Hispanic male that the informant knew. He was able to contact his source and set up the buy. He was doing this in an effort to work down his sentence.

We were able to set the deal to take place at the same location we had the command center at for the 500-kilo deal. We would do it in the parking lot. The informant was there, and we waited for the bad guy to arrive. He showed up in a newer SUV and was going to sell our informant two kilograms of cocaine. When the purchase was made, we moved in and arrested the bad guy. We placed him face down on the ground, and he had a duffle bag next to him. DEA agents were present with us because I brought them into the original case with the informant and was charging the informant federally.

When we rolled the bad guy over, the DEA Agents looked like they were in shock. The bad guy was one of their informants and was working both sides. Needless to say, they weren't very happy. It was embarrassing to an agent anytime something like that would happen. The bad guy, Juan, said that he had another twenty kilograms of cocaine inside the duffle bag and that he was going to be delivering it to a house in Pine Hills, Florida. From this two-kilogram cocaine deal, we just turned it into twenty-two kilograms.

We got the information regarding the house that Juan was going to be delivering to, and I began writing a search warrant for the house. We drove by and videotaped the outside of the residence so that we could show SWAT because they would be doing the entry. The house had burglar bars on the windows and doors, so SWAT would need a wrecker to hook a chain to the front door and pull the bars off.

I went to a judge and got the warrant signed, and we were now ready to make entry on the house. Once we were inside, I couldn't believe what I saw. The house was full of stolen merchandise that had been traded for crack cocaine. The garage was also full. The owner of the home had several microwaves in the kitchen. He was cooking up the powdered cocaine and turning it into crack cocaine. He was making millions of dollars. He had a game room in the home. I opened up a black trash bag in that room, and it had twelve thousand dollars in one-dollar bills inside of it. I opened up a pinball machine, and it had thousands of dollars inside of it. The homeowner was identified as Perry Mason. Yes, I said Perry Mason. He had moved to Florida from Alabama years prior and met a man that owned a fence company. Perry came to Florida with a first-grade education. He got into the crack cocaine business because he could make so much money at it. The owner of the fence company got involved, and he agreed to invest some of Perry's crack cocaine earnings into real estate and fancy cars. He told Perry that if he ever needed money just to let him know and he would get it for him. The fence company owner was laundering the money through his business.

I knew that Perry had a much larger sum of money in his house. Much more than what we had already found. Perry also had more than seven thousand dollars in the glove compartment of his new Z-71 pick-up truck. But that just wasn't enough. He was going to take delivery of twenty kilograms of cocaine, and he would have to pay for it. That could have cost him around four hundred thousand dollars. We went through his house with a fine-toothed comb. I knew there had to be a safe somewhere, but we just weren't finding it. We even brought in a guy with a metal detector. My sergeant was ready to call it quits, and I pled with him to just give us just a little more time. Then Mark, another fellow MBI agent, shouted from a back bedroom, "I found it." He had removed a large amount of dirty laundry from a bedroom closet then he pulled back the carpet. And there it was, a floor safe. It was the most beautiful sight I had seen that night.

I went to where Perry was sitting, and I asked him for the combination. He refused. I explained to him that it might help his case if he cooperated. He still refused and said, "My kidneys are failing, and I will die in prison anyway." He also told me that his throat had been slashed in the past while someone tried to rob him. He also told me that he had been shot in the butt. I told him that if he didn't tell me the combination, I would just call a locksmith and they would drill it.

Perry gave me the combination. When we opened the safe, it was packed full of money. I don't remember the total because it had to be taken to DEA evidence where it would be counted with a money machine. I believe the total in cash was around four hundred thousand, but DEA had the exact total. There was a great deal of very expensive jewelry as well, Rolex watches, diamond rings, diamond bracelets, and diamond necklaces.

We interviewed the owner of the fence company, and he cooperated fully in an effort as to his not going to jail. He signed over all the properties and vehicles that had been purchased with drug proceeds and was willing to testify. Agents had been trying to make a case on Perry for years for his crack cocaine trafficking and were unable to do so. On this particular day, everything just seemed to fall into place. Perry received a lengthy prison sentence, and the fence company owner later died due to health issues.

I would like to make something perfectly clear. In all my years of working drug cases, I have seen millions of dollars in drugs and illegal drug proceeds. At no time did I ever have the slightest desire to take any. To me, it was just dirty money and didn't belong to me. Anyone that could have ever been involved in doing something like that must not have thought about what it would do to their reputation, their family, or their future. I worked for everything that I have received in life, and my reputation and family were everything to me. I mentioned this because too many times I have been asked by people how I was never tempted to take some of the money and was told that nobody would have missed it or reported it missing. I would have known, and that was something I could not have lived with. I have been blessed with everything that I have earned, and there is no feeling like that.

Well, let's get on to the next case. I began looking into a subject in Orlando, Florida, that owned a used car dealership. I was getting information from a reliable source that this person was moving large amounts of cocaine through his dealership. His name was Steve. I know what you are probably thinking. Was everyone's name Steve? But the answer was no, his name was really Steve as were the others I previously mentioned.

It was time to start putting this case together and stay busy as I always had. I have been a hard worker my entire life, and my mind was always working. I got into this line of work to serve the people. That was what I was payed to do, and I was going to do it to the best of my ability.

I began gathering intelligence on Steve in an effort to learn all that I could about him. I pulled wage and hour records, I pulled sales records, I did a criminal background check on him. I ran background checks on his employees and many of his other associates. It was not looking good for Steve. He associated with a great number of people with felony drug convictions. I started pulling phone records and was able to identify more individuals that Steve was working with. Each of them had felony drug conviction backgrounds.

I had obtained enough intelligence to write a pen register. A pen register is a machine that would monitor and register all incoming and outgoing calls and document them on paper. The phone information only, not the content of the actual calls. You cannot listen to calls on a pen register. You only need reasonable suspicion to write a pen register. Reasonable suspicion is merely me using my training and experience to convince someone that the facts I listed were true and accurate. You do still need a judge to sign off on it or authorize it. From the calls that came in and went out on the pen register, you would document criminal histories of identified individuals.

All this could lead up to establishing probable cause, and that was what you needed to do what? Remember, we called it flipping the switch or rolling this case into an oral intercept case (or wiretap). Probable cause is a little more stringent than reasonable suspicion.

Probable cause means that any reasonable, or prudent, person would believe that the suspect would have committed the crime. The facts again have to be precise and exact when you present them to a judge. You don't ever want to mislead a judge or leave out any facts. If you do, you could be held liable and you could have the entire investigation thrown out. You could even be prosecuted criminally.

I got what I needed, and it was time to take it to the judge. I must have really loved hard work or maybe I just liked serving the people and bringing criminals to justice. I do know that it was time again to flip that switch because the judge signed off on it and we were good to go.

My partner, Will, would now become an integral part in this case. He would be working with me every step of the way in making this thing a success. I also had the support and assistance from my Sergeant Steve (yes, another Steve). We were up and running and gaining a great deal of intelligence in this case.

After being in the case for a while, we cultivated a confidential informant. He was an unwitting, and you remember what that means. I will refresh your memory. It means that he didn't know he was working with law enforcement. He thought that he was working with drug dealers or other bad guys. His name was Carlos. Carlos began providing us with information regarding the used car salesman Steve's cocaine operation. We were already getting intelligence from the wiretap, and Carlos was adding to it and helping confirm it without his even knowing it.

We were getting conversation about small amounts of drugs over the wire but were, however, finding that Steve, the car salesman, was a lot smarter than we had given him credit for. He had obviously been trained or coached by professionals and knew all the legalities. He had a team of lawyers working for him. He knew to not talk illegal business over the telephone. We would now have to find another way to get into his operation. We met with Carlos because Carlos had personal knowledge from working as a car detailer at car salesman Steve's used car lot. Carlos would tell us that none of the cars on the lot would ever be sold. He also said that the batteries were dead and that car salesman Steve would bid on cars at the auto auction that would have cocaine in the trunk. He would pay far more than the cars were worth if he had to, just to make sure he would get his shipment of drugs. Carlos also said that he would see car salesman Steve with large sums of cash on him and that he would always drive a Corvette.

Will and I met with Carlos one evening at a Chili's Restaurant to talk about illegal drug shipments. I told Carlos that I owned a semi-tractor and trailer and that I transported cocaine from Florida to Michigan. I told him that I had a source for my cocaine; however, I was tired of paying my sources prices. Carlos said that he may be able to help me out and he might have another source. I was presenting myself as being the money man and having the means of transporting illegal drugs. I even told Carlos I would show him my rig. Will posed as being somebody that worked for me in my illegal drug business.

During our meeting, we offered to buy Carlos a drink. Carlos told us that he couldn't drink much alcohol because of his being attacked at the fairgrounds in Orlando. He raised up his shirt and showed us where somebody had stabbed him and then cut him from below his navel all the way up through his rib cage. He said that as a result of his wounds, he lost half of his liver. His injuries were as a result of a problem with individuals he had been dealing with. We ended our meeting with Carlos and set up another time to meet so he could see my semitruck.

In the middle of this case, I was back at my office and received a phone call from my old informant, Tommy. It was a surprise because I hadn't talked to Tommy for about a year or two. And remember that I told you earlier on when I talked about Tommy and the DEA agent in Panama during the boat shipment that I would add to the story later on. That was when Tommy was told to collect $150,000.00 from the Colombians in good-faith money and he did. He met with a DEA contact agent in Panama and turned the money over to him. The DEA agent assured Tommy that there was only $130,000.00 and not the $150,000.00 that Tommy was supposed to get. Tommy assured me that he brought the $150,000.00 back to the agent and that he felt he was being threatened by the agent by telling him to agree to say there was only $130,000.00.

During this current call from Tommy, he was highly upset and very emotional, hollering at me over the phone saying, "I told you, I told you, the agent was dirty, now somebody is dead!" I tried to calm him down, telling him he was making no sense and that I didn't know what he was talking about. He went on to say the DEA special agent, Richard Fekete, that he met with in Panama, that he was dirty, and now he killed his partner. I said that I needed more detail. He said that the DEA agent had been taken out of Panama and sent back to Miami, Florida. He said that the agent shot and killed his partner in Miami and that his partner had a wife and kids. I assured Tommy that I did everything that I could when he told me about the DEA agent he had met with in Panama. I told him that I had gone to DEA authorities and gave them the information I had received from him and that they questioned my believing an informant over a federal agent. I told him after that it was out of my hands. I had done all that I could do.

Tommy told me that the story of the shooting had been released to the public in Miami and that I would be able to read about it. After my call with Tommy, I received a call from the media in Miami wanting to question me about the boat shipment case. I told the media that I was not at liberty to discuss the case and that they would need to contact DEA, seeing that it had become a federal case. The media asked me if I could at least verify whether or not the case had taken place. I said that I could because it was public record. It had been on the news, and there was an article in the *Orlando Sentinel*.

Well, I went on to do a little investigating into what happened with the two DEA agents in Miami. What I learned was that the agent, Richard Fekete, out of Panama that Tommy had alleged to be dirty, was at a Christmas party in Miami and left the party with his partner. The two were riding in the partner's car, and the agent out of Panama, Fekete, shot his partner several times, causing his death. The agent, Fekete out of Panama, used alcohol as an excuse, and he said that he blacked out. He was blaming DEA for his alcohol abuse.

I later learned after this that a DEA agent in Panama had been sent to prison for wrongdoings and another agent had been transferred. I wasn't able to identify the agent. I will never know the truth as to why DEA Agent Fekete out of Panama killed his partner; however, it is just my opinion, but I believe the deceased agent was threatening to provide authorities with incriminating information about Agent Fekete out of Panama, so he killed him. And again, that is just my theory.

The tragic thing about it all is that a possible innocent victim is dead, and he left behind a wife and children. And most likely over money or drugs.

I went on to further investigate Special Agent Fekete out of Panama and found that he did receive a fifteen-year sentence in prison followed by fifteen years' probation. I will name him in detail because it is public record. His name was DEA Special Agent Richard Fekete, I believe age fifty-five or fifty-seven at the time of the shooting. He was at a Miami Dade Christmas party on December 12, 1997, that involved more than one hundred law enforcement officers. His partner's name (the deceased) was Shaun Curl, age thirty-nine at the time of his death.

Fekete was a thirty-two-year veteran with the DEA and referred to as a ticking time bomb by the sentencing judge in the shooting case. According to the judge, friends and coworkers knew of Fekete's alcohol abuse, and nobody did anything about it. The judge felt that if it hadn't been Shaun Curl, it would have been somebody else. Fekete shot another individual in a Philadelphia bar back in 1987 while under the influence of alcohol.

In the past, Fekete also pulled a gun on his former wife, a dog, and a former partner. A previous partner of Fekete's also stated that Fekete had a problem with alcohol and other things for years, and DEA knew about it. They, however, would always give him back his gun. Agents testified at Fekete's trial that Fekete had to be carried out to Curl's car because he was so intoxicated. Curl offered to give his drunken partner a ride home. Fekete was singing, and they placed him in the car. During the ride home on an open stretch of highway through the Florida Everglades, Fekete pulled out his gun and shot Curl three times in the head and two times in the chest.

Curl's widow was not totally pleased with the sentence Fekete received. The judge could have given Fekete thirty years because the murder was that of a law enforcement officer. She was not happy that Fekete would be able to walk the streets again.

Had it been me, I would have had many more questions concerning this case. Fekete blacked out and shot his partner five times, and it was cold-blooded murder. And it was merely caused from alcohol abuse. Sorry, but I'm not buying it. I truly believe there was much more to the story. And to think that friends and coworkers knew of Fekete's problems and turned their heads the other way was unacceptable. That man's problems during his thirty-two-year career did not occur overnight. The job took its toll, and I believe that if someone had done something about his problems earlier on, instead of trying to protect his job, none of this would have happened.

I don't know if DEA does psychological testing on their agents, but I do know that at the state and local level where I worked in an undercover capacity for years, as long as we were working in undercover operations, we were tested on a pretty regular basis.

My last psychological exam occurred about a year and a half before my retirement. I was getting ready to do an undercover operation for Immigration Customs Enforcement. I was going to be the undercover agent. They required that I go through a series of psychological tests before I could engage in the operation. I had to take a lengthy written test, and then I had to go through an oral exam with ICE's staff psychologist. At the end of the exam, the psychologist told me that his findings were that I was an extreme level-headed individual and that I was resilient. It was remarkable what he could tell me about myself just from that test. I sure wish DEA could have learned some things about Fekete and done something about it.

It was time to put this behind me and get back to focusing on the case I was currently working. We were still up on the wiretap and still monitoring calls. We were getting bits of evidence but not a great deal of it. We were learning more and more how educated to the system car salesman Steve was.

Even though he was being careful on the phone, he was still giving me enough to learn his method of operation and how sophisticated his illegal drug organization was. Through intelligence gained during phone conversations, I was able to learn that car salesman Steve was linked to a car leasing company and also to a guy out of south Florida that owned an exotic high-dollar car dealership; he also owned a cigarette boat dealership and a jet airplane dealership. I even uncovered information about that guy that indicated he owned a functional submarine. The guy did have a criminal history for drug trafficking. DEA actually had intelligence about subjects bringing cocaine out of Colombia and into the United States inside of a submarine.

I also learned about the leasing company's method of operation. Car dealership Steve would actually purchase high-end exotic cars from the guy in south Florida. Steve would then pay the leasing company for a bogus lease for each vehicle. That way, Steve knew that if the driver of any of the vehicles hauling drugs were stopped by police, they couldn't seize the vehicle because it was registered as a lease vehicle.

I needed to, as we say, put drugs on the table. Will agreed to go to car salesman Steve's dealership and make a drug purchase. He was able to buy 3 ounces of cocaine from Carlos at the dealership. This was a good thing; however, we couldn't link Steve to the sale. We couldn't prove that he had knowledge that the deal took place, so we had physical dope but still not a whole bunch to incriminate Steve.

I learned over the wiretap that Steve was having a party at his home. Steve had a house in Orlando that really stood out. It took up most of the block and was just so much more elaborate than any of the other homes in the neighborhood. I got with Carlos and checked to see if I could go to the party. Carlos was able to get me the invitation, so a female agent from MBI and myself attended the party. I was really hoping to build some kind of rapport with Steve while at his party.

I was driving a new Mitsubishi 3000 GT and really playing the role as a high-level drug dealer. Steve had his own band, and he was the drummer. I struck up a conversation with him and actually got up on stage with his band and sang. I thought things went very well. I talked with Carlos at the party and now had him convinced to step up the game and start dealing with me by providing kilograms of cocaine.

Carlos was still insistent on seeing my truck. I was able to connect with a company out of south Orlando that was willing to lend me a Peterbilt tractor and a dry box trailer. Remember, I used to drive truck cross country for a living, so that was really helping my undercover role. I was able to talk the talk about being from nearly anywhere. I also kept my commercial driver's license up-to-date.

I parked the rig at a truck stop in south Orlando off of Hwy. 441. I had Carlos meet me there and convinced him that I had stopped at the truck stop for the night and slept in my sleeper after a trip. The name of my company was North/South Trucking. I even had an undercover office with signs in the window that said North/South Trucking.

Carlos was very pleased with my operation and agreed to set up a supplier for my cocaine trafficking operation. Carlos contacted me several days later and said that he had somebody out of south Florida that wanted to supply me with cocaine. I told Carlos that I would be interested in doing something but not on a large scale, maybe three kilos of cocaine to start. I told him that I wanted to build a trusted working relationship with these guys and then we could talk about larger scale deals in the future. Carlos agreed.

Carlos contacted me the next day and said that his source could do it but that we would have to do the deal at his house. We normally would never do that because of agent safety issues and also, you are giving the bad guys too much control.

We had a major briefing at the MBI office with agents and command staff to discuss whether or not to go through with this. The agreement was made to move forward. Will and I drove the Mitsubishi 3000 GT to Carlos's residence that was located on Turrisi Blvd. in Orlando, Florida. Our purpose for going was to do what we call a surprise money flash. We met with Carlos at his home and discussed how the deal for the 3 kilograms of cocaine was going to happen. We were leaving, and Carlos walked us out to the car. As I was getting ready to drive off, I told Carlos that I wanted to show him something. I opened up a duffle bag that contained $50,000.00 and showed it to him. Carlos had a look of surprise, and said, "I knew you were good for it, let's make this happen." Then Will and I drove off with the money.

In an undercover operation like this, you don't ever want the money and drugs to come together. And the reason I say this is because in an intense situation, the money would be your strongest weapon. You will see what I mean by that as we get deeper into this story. The money would now become my savior.

The money flash and the meeting went well with Carlos. I knew that after Carlos saw that much money, he would be burning up his source's telephone. The following morning, I got a call from Carlos. He told me that he had spoken to his source and that his source would have to travel to Miami, Florida, to hook up with his contact and pick up the three kilos of cocaine. Carlos said that they would be able to do the three-kilo deal later on that same evening.

We held another briefing that involved MBI command staff, fellow MBI supervisors, MBI agents, and SWAT command staff. My Sergeant Steve was brand new to the unit and being thrown in to this thing as the on-scene supervisor. He would be in charge of running the deal from the outside. It seemed pretty unfair to him, but he was up for the challenge. There were discussions about placing two snipers in front of the target residence in an open grassy area across the street from Carlos's residence. A SWAT rescue team would occupy an unmarked panel van.

There were detailed questions being asked of me by MBI command staff. I was asked that if this thing went bad, how did I want them to handle it. They asked if I was held captive by the bad guys, did I want them to rush the house, flash bang it with a concussion grenade, and conduct a rescue. Or did I want them to hold off and treat it as a hostage situation and negotiate with the bad guys.

I told them that if this thing went bad, I wanted them to come in, bang the house, and take down every bad guy in there. I knew what the bad guys were capable of, and I knew that a human life didn't mean much to them. I told MBI command staff that if I was going to die in that house, I would rather do it looking at a friendly face and not one of the bad guys. They also asked me whether or not I wanted my partner, Will, to go in with me. I told them that if this thing did go bad, I would rather the bad guys had one hostage and not two. I also told them that I had a lot more experience than Will, and I would not jeopardize his life.

I didn't realize how important all this was going to be. I have been in some very intense situations throughout my career; however, I was about to experience the most challenging, dangerous, and stressful situation I had ever been in. This was going to be a time that I would have to put my experience, training, street smarts, and gift of gab to the ultimate test. I later learned that MBI command had some information that had not been shared with me, and I will share that information later on.

Something very critical about an operation such as this was that whatever the undercover agent, the rescue team, and command staff agrees upon, that plan has to be followed to the letter. I say this because the undercover agent is put under so much pressure, and he has enough to focus on when dealing with the bad guys, you can't throw a wrench into the mix and add to the undercover agent's problem at hand. He has it in his mind the way things are supposed to go down, and then if something happens, that changes that, he has to regroup and not only focus on his survival, but he now has to try and figure out what his team's next move would be. It can be overwhelming and totally not necessary. You will learn why soon.

Well, now everything was in place. We would have two armed snipers in front of the target location in ghillie suits. That is a form of camouflage. We would have MBI agents assisting with surveillance. We would have a SWAT team in a panel van for agent rescue purposes. Will and I would act as the undercover agents. I would be the undercover agent, and Will would be with me acting as the person in control of the money.

I got a call from Carlos at about 3:00 p.m. Carlos told me that him and his source was on their way back to Orlando from Miami and that they would be ready to do the deal by around 7:00 p.m. I agreed, and we put the plan to action. Carlos called me back around 6:30 p.m. and said that they were ready. I got the rescue team set up near a Steak and Ale located off Hwy 50 in Orlando near the target residence. MBI agents also got set up in the area. The snipers got into place at the target location on Turrisi Blvd.

We put Will in the director of MBI's Jeep SUV with the $50,000.00. I got into the Mitsubishi 3000 GT. I called Carlos, and now I gave him the location being that of the Steak and Ale, and I told him to meet us there. It is always good for you to pick the location and give it last minute so that the bad guys don't have the time to put counter surveillance in place. Will had a cover team from MBI following him to protect him and the money.

We pulled into the Steak and Ale and went inside. Carlos was there with two Hispanic males (the other two bad guys). We sat at a table and discussed whether or not this thing was going to happen. I was wired with two separate devices so that my cover team could listen and record conversations.

Carlos's source whom identified himself to me as Louis seemed to be the guy in charge. Louis spoke fluent English; however, his partner, Ernesto, did not. Ernesto seemed fresh into the United States. Louis told me that him and Ernesto had driven to Miami earlier in the day with Carlos accompanying them, and they picked up the three kilos of cocaine that I was going to buy from them. This seemed believable to me because earlier in the day, I received a call from Carlos that came from a Miami number. I was asked by Louis several times if I had the money. I kept telling him that the money was nearby and that I showed it to Carlos and that Carlos knew that I was good for it.

If you remember as I said previously, the money can be your only means of protection, and you never want the money and drugs to come together. You will soon see what I meant by that.

I was also asked by command staff if I was going to be armed when I was involved in the cocaine transaction. I told them no. And I will tell you this. The undercover agent is the one that puts his butt on the line, and that should be his or her choice.

I saw a training video once that was an actual deal that took place between bad guys and a DEA agent inside of the bad guy's residence. The agent doing the deal was armed. When he met with one bad guy outside in the front yard, you could see him and hear him talking with the bad guy. The agent had done several previous deals with that bad guy, and now he was ready to do a major buy. The bad guy kept asking the agent if he had the money, and the agent kept avoiding the question, and he didn't say anything about where the money was. The bad guy asked the agent to pull up his shirt because he wanted to see if he was wired. You could hear how nervous and uneasy the agent was due to his heavy breathing, and you could also hear it in his voice.

The agent said to the bad guy, "We have done a lot of business together, why are you asking me to do that?"

The bad guy said, "Just do it."

The agent's gut was telling him something was wrong, but he just wasn't listening. In this line of work, there is a lot of peer pressure and you want to make the deal happen. Well, the DEA agent raised his shirt, and you could see his gun fall to the ground. He nervously reached down and picked it up. The bad guy asked him what he was doing with the gun. The agent said "I am just looking out for myself" and he said to the bad guy, "You would do the same thing." The bad guy agreed and then told the agent to follow him inside the home.

Once they got inside the residence you could no longer see the agent and the bad guy; however, you could still hear the audio, and their conversations were being recorded. Over the device, you could hear an echo, and you heard the agent ask the bad guy where all his furniture was. It sounded like things were getting bad. The bad guy said that he had to sell all his furniture. Then you could hear the agent ask the bad guy where his family was. You see, during previous deals, the bad guy always had his family present. The bad guy said that he sent them off someplace. Then you could hear a two-way radio in the background, and it was the voice of another bad guy doing counter surveillance. He was asking the bad guy in the house to ask the agent who the person was driving around in a brown Thunderbird. The brown Thunderbird was occupied by another DEA agent who was acting as part of a cover team. And remember what I said when your cover was blown? He just got burned. Now the agent had added stress having to come up with an answer. He was really getting nervous now and tried to find a response. The bad guy asked him again where the money was. The agent put him off again and said that it was nearby. The agent was feeling all kinds of pressure now, and it just didn't sound like he had a backup plan.

The bad guy pressured him one more time and said, "Where is the money?"

The agent broke down and said, "The money was in the trunk of his car."

The minute that happened, a closet door opened from within the house, and another bad guy came out and struck the agent with a baseball bat. You could now hear the agent was screaming and begging for his life. He had just lost all control because he gave up his strongest weapon. Now the bad guy pulled the agent's gun out of his waistband and put the gun in the agent's mouth. You could hear the muffled sound of the agent begging, telling the bad guy to not kill him and that he had a family. What an extremely horrible thing to have to listen to.

I would never criticize the agent's actions that day, but I will share some observations. I again feel that the money and drugs should never come together in a drug operation. The money was what the bad guys wanted. Once they had it, his life meant nothing. The agent brought the gun to the deal and provided it. He was in a situation where he became overpowered, and the gun became more of a detriment than a weapon, and now it was being used against him. None of the bad guys had guns, and the agent was in a contained environment. When you are outnumbered and captured by the element of surprise, it is very tough to defend against. If you try to react with mutual force, you are likely to get shot anyway. Unless you are Steven Segal or Chuck Norris.

Things were very bad, and I will just continue by saying the agent did survive because when the cover team came to attempt an agent rescue, the bad guys, fortunately for the agent, decided to flee instead of kill him. This incident destroyed the agent's career, and he quit shortly thereafter. I wish I could say all this could have been avoided, but I can't. But I will say thank you to the agent because as a result of this, a great deal was learned.

Let's get back to what was about to happen with me. Louis and I agreed on the price for the cocaine, and we were ready to drive to Carlos's house and do the deal. As we all walked out to our cars, I asked Louis to walk over to the Jeep SUV that Will was driving. I opened the rear hatch, and I opened the duffle bag that had the $50,000.00 in it, and I showed the money to Louis. Louis said that he recognized the SUV as being one that kept driving past Carlos's house all day long. At the time, I didn't know what he was talking about, but I had to come up with a response quick. I told Louis that yes it was me and that I was checking things out to make sure everything was ok. I told him that he would have done the same thing if he were in my shoes, and he agreed. I learned later on that it had actually been the director of MBI that had been driving by without my knowledge. His actions caused me to have to think quickly on my feet yet another time. I then had Will drive off with the money, and there was an MBI cover team that would follow him and the money for protection purposes.

I got into the Mitsubishi 3000 GT, and Carlos approached me. He asked me if he could ride with me to the house, and he said Louis and Ernesto would follow in another vehicle. I agreed and told him to get into the passenger side. Once he was inside the car, I began to drive out of the parking lot. There was a Dairy Queen next door to the Steak and Ale, and my SWAT rescue team van was parked in the lot between other cars. It was just a plain-looking white van, and I didn't even notice it.

Carlos immediately said, "Hey, what's with that van?"

I said "What van, Carlos?" and he said, "That white one, it is sitting very low to the ground."

I guess SWAT team members carry some weight with all that gear and everything. I told Carlos that he was very paranoid and he needed to relax. I also told him that he was making me uneasy and that we didn't have to do this deal. I told him that if it was risky, I didn't need to do it because I already had a source for my cocaine. I thought to myself that Carlos was not the smartest guy, but he had some street smarts, and he was very observant.

I drove out onto Highway 50 in Orlando and had to wait in the middle lane until traffic cleared. Louis and Ernesto pulled up next to me, and Carlos began speaking to them in Spanish. At the time, my Spanish was not good at all, and I wish it was. They were obviously talking about the van, and Louis and Ernesto told Carlos that they would go one way and we should go another to see if any of us were being followed. Was there something I was missing in regards to being cautious? Were there signs that I was missing? I still wasn't getting that gut feeling. I had done deals like this in the past, and there were things that happened that were similar. Nothing highly unusual had happened yet. Paranoia was always pretty much a common behavior for drug dealers.

I pulled up to Carlos's residence and made sure that I parked three houses down so that I would give my snipers a clear view of the front of the home. Carlos and I walked inside, and we went to the dining room area. When we walked in the house, the movie *Speed* was playing on the television. It was at the scene where the discussion was taking place to kill the hostage. I made a comment about that and we laughed. Who was to know that I was eventually going to become a hostage?

A moment later, Louis and Ernesto entered the residence carrying a blue duffle bag, and they came into the dining room. Ernesto threw the bag on the table, and Louis said that the bag contained the three kilos of cocaine. I told Louis that I wanted to remove one of the kilos and test it. He seemed surprised. That was my first gut feeling that something was not right. Louis agreed, but he didn't seem anxious about doing so. I carried a small bottle of cobalt with me, and I took it out. Carlos handed me a knife from the kitchen drawer, and I cut into one package. I put a small amount of cocaine on the end of the knife and I placed a drop of cobalt on it. If the substance was cocaine, it would have turned blue. When the cobalt hit it, nothing happened. Now I knew I was in trouble. My take down signal was "It looks good," and I gave the signal immediately. My distress signal was, "This stuff is shit." I gave that signal immediately, and I was looking at Louis when I said it.

Louis said to me, "No, try another package."

I knew I had to stall for time to allow the team to get ready to respond, so I took out a second package and cut into it. When I started to place a drop of cobalt on it, Louis instantly placed a 9mm handgun in my right ear, and he pulled me down to my knees. Ernesto was pointing a .357 Magnum at my forehead. This was a rip. They wanted to kill me and take the money. They never expected me to test the suspected cocaine. They assumed that I would just accept the drugs and hand over the $50,000.00. I was waiting to hear a flash bang concussion grenade and hear SWAT making entry; however, that didn't happen. Louis told me to get on my cellular phone and call Will and tell him to bring the money. Louis pulled up my jacket to check me for a weapon and to see if I was wired. I told Louis that I couldn't do that. Louis said again for me to make the call. I said I couldn't, and then I decided to try and cause problems between Louis, Ernesto, and Carlos, so I began shouting at Carlos saying I thought you said these guys were ok and told him that I trusted him and now this.

Carlos started yelling at Louis, and he said, "Don't kill him in my house."

My plan worked briefly because Louis turned his gun towards Carlos and he said to Ernesto, "Let's kill that motherf——r!"

Carlos ran down the hall and slammed a bedroom door behind him. Then I heard glass breaking. Carlos jumped right through the window, and he was off and running. What I didn't know was that there was another male sleeping in the bedroom. He urinated on the bed, and he was off and running too. Part of the MBI cover team captured Carlos in a convenience store parking lot. My undercover name was Brian during this undercover deal as well, and Carlos kept saying to MBI cover team members, "They were going to kill Brian, you have to help him, they are going to kill Brian." Carlos still didn't know I was a cop.

Louis and Ernesto now turned their focus back on me. I had found myself in the most helpless situation I had ever been in. I had been shot at, I had fought bad guys over guns, I was in too many foot pursuits with armed suspects to mention, and now I was in a position with two armed gunmen that wanted to kill me, and I had no means to fight back. Or did I? I still had something they wanted very badly.

The money! If they killed me, then there would be no money. I am going to call the rest of what I was about to do, using brains over brawn. I didn't need to have to use outer physical strength, instead I needed a greater power of inner intelligence.

I had to somehow outsmart them. It would be difficult to do if I didn't remain calm and think. Believe me, it wasn't easy to do under the violent circumstances I was facing. I really felt that these guys wanted to kill me. I always knew that the longer that I stayed in this line of work, this type of possibility existed and that this could happen.

Louis had me remain on my knees. I was getting more and more angry because I truly had a feeling of helplessness. During every other stressful or violent situation that I had found myself in through the years, I could always fight back physically. But not this time. I had to do something and do it fast. My team was not coming.

Louis put the gun in my right ear again, and he pulled the hammer back. It does not take a lot of pressure to be placed on the trigger of a semiautomatic to make the weapon discharge, and I knew that. Louis said for me to get Carlos back there. I said to Louis, "Just how do you expect me to do that?" This made me think now, just how well did Carlos really know these guys if they were depending on me to get him back?

Louis told me to make the call to Will and get the money brought there or he would kill me, and I kept telling him that I can't do that. Then Louis said something that really surprised me. He said, "Oh yeah, he left his phone at the bar."

Will must have accidently left his phone at the bar, and Louis saw it but I didn't. This may sound like it was a bad thing, but it turned out to be a good thing. Because now Louis believed me when I said I couldn't call Will. Louis shoved the gun into my ear one more time, and that was it. I had taken all that I could from him, and I thought that I would not die without a fight. I didn't want my family or coworkers to hear that I had been shot in the head while being on my knees. I got up and turned towards Louis, and I actually backed him up against the wall where he had to raise the gun up against his chest.

I said, "Damn it, Louis, I told you we have to go to the money."

Will and I had a plan, and part of it was that he would not come here. I was starting to lose my composure, and then something, a spirit, an angel, or someone in the room seemed to tap me on the shoulder and say, "Think, think about what you are doing." I know you have probably heard that before, and you may be skeptical about believing it, but it did happen. When your mind is under that kind of duress, it is very difficult to think clearly. Somebody or something was in that room that night watching over me. Thank God they were because I looked over at Ernesto whom I had momentarily forgotten about, and he was pointing the .357 at me with his finger on the trigger and his hand was trembling. He wanted to shoot me.

I said "Ok, ok" and I paused. But that was the move that finally got them to take me outside.

We began walking towards the front door of Carlos's house, and Louis and Ernesto followed behind me with guns pointed at my back. I was still thinking, *Where was my team? Where was my help. Were they outside waiting? Would they be there when we walked outside?* I just didn't know. I had done my part to make things as safe as I could for all people involved, and that was to get the bad guys outside.

Well, I had my hands raised in the air because that was a signal to your back up units or assisting agents that you have a gun or guns pointed at you. Believe me, that night, my hands were raised so high my fingertips were touching the clouds.

They got me to their car that was parked in Carlos's driveway. Ernesto went to the driver's side, and Louis had me at the passenger's side, still pointing his gun at me. I looked around inconspicuously and didn't see any movement or any sign of help or rescue team present. I knew that the two snipers were in the field across the street, so I tried to speak loud enough for them to hear what I was saying. I know you must be thinking where was my help. I still didn't know at this point, and I would try to learn later.

Well, now Louis told me to get into the rear passenger's side of the car. I had plenty enough training and experience to know that I was not getting in that car, and I refused to. If this thing was going to end, I was going to make it end right there. There was no way that I was getting into the car that they had control of and then leave myself and my rescue team with no control.

Louis said once again "Get in the car" and I said no. I kept trying to stall to give my team time to get there or for my sniper to be given the order to take the shot. I later learned that the sniper had been given the green light to take the shot; however, he did not shoot. Then Louis told me to get into the front passenger's side of the car or he was going to kill me, and I said, "Look, Louis, if I am not going to get into the back seat, why would you think that I would get into the front seat?"

Louis seemed confused as if he had never been told no before when he was holding a gun on somebody. I still didn't see anyone coming and had to come up with another way to keep his mind off shooting me. I had about $125.00 on me, and I handed it to him and said, "Take this money, money don't mean anything to me." I raised my voice in an effort to be saying to my sniper "Shoot this guy, he is getting ready to shoot me." In my mind, I was thinking about how a person gets shot and how they were hit first and then you hear the gunshot. I was thinking that if the sniper shot Louis, what would I do, and I knew that I would grab his gun and fight Ernesto.

Well, still no shot fired and still no rescue team. I believe to this day that an angel stayed with me because Louis was running out of patience. I should have been shot, but somebody or something stopped him from pulling the trigger. I was running out of stall tactic ideas Then all of a sudden, I saw a white van coming down the road towards us. I recognized the van as being the same van that was in the Dairy Queen parking lot with SWAT members in it earlier. Louis was standing where his back was to the van, and Ernesto was standing on the side of the car where he would be closest to the van's approach.

When I looked past Louis's shoulder in the direction of the van, Louis noticed me and said, "Who is that?"

I said, "I don't know, Louis, it is just somebody driving by."

I told him to lower his gun so that they didn't see it. I knew that I had the car between me and Ernesto and that SWAT rescue would approach him first. Now there was only one gunman to deal with. Louis lowered his gun and the van stopped, and SWAT members exited. I put my left hand out to block Louis's hand from raising his gun again, and I punched him in the face, knocking him down. The money I gave him and his gun fell on the ground beside him. I jumped on him and struck him several more times. My stress level had reached the maximum, and he wasn't going to point that gun at me again. SWAT secured Ernesto and then came and took control of Louis, and I remember somebody saying "Ok, Rodney, ok, Rodney" and they pulled me away and put me in the director of MBI's SUV. For this case, I received the International Narcotics Officers Association's Medal of Valor, the Orange County Sheriff's Office Medal of Valor, and a Combat Ribbon.

There was a large awards ceremony held in West Palm Beach, Florida, and the head of the Drug Enforcement Administration presented me with the International Narcotics Officers Medal of Valor.

When MBI agents searched the car that Louis and Ernesto tried to place me in, they discovered a 223 rifle with a functional grenade launcher on it, plastic, and duct tape to wrap my body in and all that was in the trunk. They placed the two bad guys in the back of a patrol car and recorded their conversation. They discussed killing another subject after another drug deal had gone bad. They spoke of where the car was located where they had transported his body in. Police went to that address and found the car and evidence of a large amount of blood in the rear seat.

Carlos was later questioned and admitted to being paid by Louis for him to try and clean the blood up; however, Carlos said that there was so much blood that it was nearly impossible. We learned that a young man was killed by this group during a drug deal. They shot him multiple times in the head. Well, it was finally over. Or was it?

Things continued to happen. I found out later that the director of MBI had received a phone call from one of his informants. The caller told the director that he had picked up a conversation over a cordless phone where two males were discussing a drug deal they were about to get involved in, and they said that they were going to kill the person they were going to be dealing with and take his money. That call took place before I was going to do my deal, and I was never told about it. And it was supposed to happen in the Orlando, Florida, area.

Then the day that I went back to work, I was approached by our elevator lady. I knew her because she had been working in the building for some time. Her name was Sharon, and she was very religious. She said to me that she had a strong urge to pray for me the same evening my drug deal took place. I asked her if she had spoken with anybody about me, and she said she had not. She asked me if I was ok, and she said that she was really concerned about me. She said that God had spoken to her. That was just the beginning. Other unanswered things continued to happen.

One of my fellow agents in MBI (George) came to me when he saw me in the office, and he said that the night of my drug deal, he was on his way to church. He said that he felt a strong urge to pull his car over and pray for me, so he did. I couldn't understand why the bad guys didn't kill me that night, but I feel that I was beginning to understand. I was feeling that God was answering their prayers and that he still had a plan for me.

Sometime later, I met with the homicide investigators that were working the case against Louis and Ernesto. They had interviewed the two of them, and they kept telling me how lucky I was to be alive. Louis and Ernesto told the investigators about their plans to kill me. I feel that my experience and training helped me tremendously that night, and by remaining calm, I never lost control, but I do believe that there was a much more powerful being in that house with me that night. I really feel that had it not been for God, I would have been shot.

Then the court proceedings began. The defendants were actually taking this thing to trial, and it would become a worse nightmare for me than the actual hostage taking. And each evening when I would return to the office after court, I would run into Sharon, the elevator operator. She would tell me that I was not listening to God. She told me that he was trying to speak to me in the early morning hours and that I needed to listen. It was so strange because I had been waking up every night around 2:00 a.m. or 3:00 a.m., and I would have trouble going back to sleep.

I decided to take the promotional test and make the effort to become a supervisor. I went through the process and did very well. I scored 100 on the practical portion and 96 on the written resume portion, which was the highest score out of 118 applicants. I was later promoted to corporal.

Back to the trial. I was subpoenaed to attend a deposition regarding the case. A deposition is where you are questioned by the defense in an effort for them to obtain information that they can use against you at trial. They really raked me over the coals and kept me in the room for a very long period of time. It was an extremely stressful experience, almost as bad as the original ordeal I had just gone through. At one time, I got up and walked out and told the prosecutor that was present that I did not have to stand for the kind of treatment I was experiencing. I told her that I was not the bad guy, I was the victim.

I honestly thought that the night of my encounter with the armed gunmen was the worst time of my life; however, the worst was yet to come. In the courtroom, I was on the witness stand for hours each day over a period of several days. I was badgered by more than one attorney time and time again. I was truly feeling like the bad guy. Then during the trial, two homicide investigators showed up to testify. I knew these detectives and thought that they were there to testify on my behalf. Man, was I wrong. They were there to ask for leniency for the real bad guys, Louis, Ernesto, and Carlos. They apparently cut a deal with the bad guys in return for information. They were not sharp enough to realize that the information they received was public knowledge and posted in the newspaper. The bad guys actually didn't give them anything that they could not have gotten on their own. I was furious.

We needed informants in police work, that was for sure. We, however, needed to be selective about which ones we were willing to cut deals with.

I testified about the murder these guys committed when they killed the young man by shooting him in the head. During one of the recess periods, I was in the men's bathroom, and I was approached by that young man's father. He began shouting at me and saying, "What is going on in that courtroom?" He said, "I admit my son was a drug dealer, but he didn't deserve to die the way that he did. These guys deserve to die."

I was taken back by all of it and explained to him. I said, "Aren't you listening? I am a victim too. I put these guys away and nearly lost my life doing it. How do you think I feel?"

He settled down and apologized to me.

Then my agency held a crisis debriefing and brought everyone together that was involved the night of the incident. Even the communication centers dispatchers. Everyone that played a part was there. Some cried and let out their emotions and were able to speak about the effects it had on them. The sniper and I talked, and we hugged. He broke down and said that he was sorry, but he just couldn't take the shot. In order for us to get through the rest of our careers, I said, "Look, I didn't like the shoes I was wearing that night as well as I am sure you didn't like the ones you had on. Everyone went home safely and the bad guys went to jail."

That was a perfect ending according to our system. But now being truthful, I have to honestly say I wish he would have shot Louis. Because I was aware of all the harm Louis had done throughout the years, and I knew that he would eventually get out of prison and do it again.

The bad guys got sentenced and didn't receive near enough time in jail as far as I was concerned. In fact, they are all already back on the streets. I think Louis did the most time out of the three of them by serving about twelve years.

A funny thing occurred towards the end of the trial. When I was leaving the witness stand and I was all finished with my testimony, Carlos shouted out to me from the defendant's box, "Hey, Brian, will you save that job for me with your trucking company until after I get out of prison?"

He must not have been listening when I was being sworn in and I identified myself by my real name and as a law enforcement officer. It just goes to show you just how smart these guys really were.

This had all occurred in the mid-1990s when cocaine was at an all-time high coming into the country. Then we received information from the FBI that we possibly had a bad cop within the Orange County Sheriff's Office and they were asking for help. We learned that the cop was a police captain with Orange County and that he was doing immoral things.

According to the FBI, he was providing protection for the local drug dealers and extorting them out of money. He was also tipping them off when we would execute drug search warrants. I got a call from the captain one afternoon, and he was very inquisitive about our operations in MBI. I had to maintain my composure because I have to say that he made me furious. I had almost lost my life previously in the line of duty, and now a dirty cop was trying to get information from me about our drug operations so he could give it to the drug dealers in exchange for cash. Nobody hates a dirty cop more than a good cop. I would be glad to assist in getting him off the streets.

The FBI ended up getting a tip from a car dealership owner in Orlando, Florida, that the Orange County captain was putting pressure on. The dealership owner admitted that he was involved in the illegal drug business and that the captain was pressuring him to pay for protection. The dealership owner said that he couldn't take anymore and that he wanted to help put the dirty cop behind bars.

The car dealership owner said that the Orange County captain was pressing him for a payment immediately or else he would shut his business down. The decision was made to offer the captain a vehicle for payment instead of cash. The dealership owner told him that business had been slow and that he really didn't have money at the time. A newer sport utility vehicle was offered, and the captain agreed to accept. What a huge break for all of us. The FBI used the MBI tech unit to install video and audio equipment in the SUV, and things couldn't have turned out better. The Orange County captain used the SUV to travel to Miami, Florida, to pick up kilograms of cocaine, and all of it was captured on video and audio. It proved to be a strong case against him. The captain was charged and convicted and was sent to prison. The man had a family and a very promising career with the Orange County Sheriff's Office, and he threw it all away. As you can see with all this that bad cops are not tolerated and are punished for their wrongdoings.

After this, I learned that there was a case going on in New Orleans, Louisiana, involving numbers of bad cops that were on the New Orleans Police Department. The FBI initiated that case and gave it the name Operation Shattered Shield. The bad cop's method of operation was very similar to the case involving the Orange County Sheriff's captain.

They, too, were extorting drug dealers and forcing them to pay for protection in exchange for thousands of dollars in cash. The FBI was able to insert an undercover agent and make a strong case against the dirty cops. The dirty cop that was overseeing everything and basically in charge was recruiting other cops from within the department, and they were receiving payments as well.

At one point during the operation, a female citizen came forward and made a complaint against a couple of the cops for police brutality. She had witnessed one of the cop's pistol whip one of the youths in the neighborhood. The complaint enraged the dirty cop in charge because it was bringing heat down on them from within the department. As a result of this, he ordered a hit on the female to shut her up. The hit man was paid a measly three hundred dollars to shoot and kill her. This was a law-abiding citizen with children trying to help get the neighborhood she lived in straight. Now she was murdered, and it was orchestrated by a man that had taken an oath to protect her. It sickens me.

If it is any consolation, all the officers involved were arrested and convicted. They all received lengthy prison sentences. The dirty cop in charge received the death penalty for his involvement in the murder of the innocent female victim. The jury only deliberated for fifteen minutes after the trial and returned with a verdict of guilty. The death penalty conviction was later overturned, and he received life in prison without no eligibility for parole. The New Orleans Police Chief was replaced.

Bad behavior of police is not tolerated, and the few that are bad are dealt with. And it is a small amount considering the number of police there are nationwide. Each agency has an Internal Affairs Division that monitors the behavior of their officers. A use of force form would have to be completed in our agency for every use of force performed. The Internal Affairs Division would review the forms to decide whether or not the use of force was proper.

Police shootings would be investigated by the Florida Department of Law Enforcement. As you can see, there are things in place to closely monitor police activity, and I have only named a few. There was also a citizen's review board that would monitor police behavior.

There are hundreds of thousands of medical malpractice cases annually, and how much of it do you hear on the news? People in the medical profession are protected through medical malpractice insurance. There have actually been doctors that have intentionally misdiagnosed patients just for financial gain. I have never seen rioting or protesting as a result of their actions.

Please don't misunderstand what I am saying. I would never excuse or condone the bad behavior of a cop. However, what I am doing is trying to detail a great deal of things that are overlooked. A cop risks his or her life every time they leave their home. When the World Trade Center Towers were under a cowardly attack by terrorists, good cops (great cops) ran towards the buildings to save lives and risk their own. When the Boston Marathon bombs were detonated by cowardly terrorists, the heroic Boston cops risked their lives to save lives. The Watertown cops were some of the greatest heroes I have ever witnessed. They were fearless in protecting their community and taking the remaining bad guy into custody.

Now it was time for me to decide whether or not I should remain in narcotics or would this be a good time to take a break from it. The Orange County Sheriff's Office was starting up community policing, and they were forming a mountain bike unit. I decided to put in for a position with the unit in the Apopka area (Sector 1), and I got it. I was the assistant supervisor in the unit, and it was quite different being back in a uniform and a marked patrol car.

I began learning just how quickly the respect for law enforcement had disappeared. People just weren't acting the same, and they were very abusive with their language and hand gestures. It was becoming more stressful than drug work.

One evening, I was working at the Embassy nightclub in Orlando, Florida. It was an off-duty job where I could work and make some extra money on my off night from my regular work. I was riding through the parking lot on my mountain bike, and two females were approaching me. One of them said to me, "I think somebody is trying to steal that car over there." I thanked them and asked them to just keep walking to get them out of harm's way.

I noticed one of the turn signals flashing on the car, and I could see two people inside the front seat. I rode up to get a closer look, and I could see them both leaning over the steering wheel as if to be breaking the ignition on the column. I ordered them both out at gunpoint. They could only exit the car from the driver's side due to the passenger side being against a fence. One of the male subjects laid down on the ground, and the second subject used him as a shield then ran away. I secured the one subject in handcuffs and tried to get the attention of other deputies over the radio that were working the front door of the club. An SUV pulled up to where I was at, and the occupants asked if I needed help. I asked them to please go and tell deputies at the door of the Embassy that I needed assistance, and they did. A deputy came to assist; however, we never got the other subject. The steering column on the car had been broken, and they were just about ready to drive off with the car. I was so grateful to all the citizens that assisted that night.

A young deputy named John that worked that zone would stop by and see me on the evenings that I worked at the Embassy lounge. He had just left a little while before this incident to answer a call for service. John was a great young man, and he was learning the job quick. He was just a great, caring young man, and he was a good cop.

John was responding to a call for service where a deputy needed help, and John's patrol car was struck by a semitruck, killing him instantly. This was a tragic loss for his family, his friends, and his fellow deputies. John will be truly missed by all.

I had another off-duty job that I worked in order to make ends meet, and on a cop's salary, I worked many. It was a Saturday night. That evening, I was working security covering five car dealerships on Colonial Dr. in Orlando, Florida. I had to work all night. Cops work very irregular hours, weekends, and holidays. That's why many marriages don't last. On that particular night, I saw a car on the side of Colonial Dr., with its emergency flashers on. I pulled over to see if I could assist. The driver was a Middle Eastern male, and his Middle Eastern wife was in the passenger's seat. They had suffered a flat tire, and the male couldn't get the lug nuts off. I offered to help. They were two very hardworking individuals. They did janitorial work all night at office buildings. I was able to remove the lug nuts and remove the flat tire; however, the spare tire to the car was flat. I offered to drive the Middle Eastern male to the service station and get air in his spare tire. He accepted, and we had his wife remain in the car with the doors locked. When we got to the station, the man told me that he didn't have any money, so I paid to put air in his spare tire. He was extremely grateful, and I got him and his wife back on the road so that they could get home.

There was something about all this that really got to me. You see that night, I was driving an unmarked pick-up truck, I was wearing plain street clothes, and never told the couple I was a policeman. They took the time and effort to find out who I was and contacted a local radio program. They gave them my name and told the program what I had done. In return, the program gave me an award for Police Officer of the Week, and they provided me with dinner for two at a very exclusive restaurant where they had someone there to honor me. A humorous thing about that was when the radio station called me to tell me that I was being honored, I thought that it was some kind of a joke. Police officers were constantly playing jokes on one another just to help deal with the tragic things they often encountered. I thought it was another cop playing a joke on me. I hung up on the caller. He called back and was able to convince me that it was for real.

That was one of the most rewarding honors I had ever received. Just the thought of those two going to the trouble that they had to honor me was outstanding. A little kindness can go a long way. This was proof.

Tragic events were just continually happening around me. Was it a message, or was it just part of the job? But it was happening while I was off duty as well. One evening, while out at dinner at a Don Pablo's, a large group of people were enjoying dinner together. One large man at the table began choking profusely. The woman next to him raised his arm up, and I saw it drop to the table. Then I saw the man fall face first into his mashed potatoes. He was unconscious.

My wife and I were still married at the time, and she looked at me and said, "Oh no, not again." I got up and went over to the large man and checked to see if he was conscious. He was not. I lifted him from behind, and I began performing the Heimlich maneuver on him several times. All of a sudden, a large piece of steak expelled from inside of his mouth, and he began gasping for air. I asked him if he needed medical attention, and he said that he would be alright.

I returned to my table and saw my ex-wife crying. I asked her what was wrong, and she said, "This always happens to you."

Two young girls were sitting across from us, and I could hear one girl say to the other "He did that" and she pointed at me.

An elderly gentleman said to me "Hey, son, way to go" and he gave me a thumbs up.

Our waiter came over and said that he wouldn't be charging us for our drinks. I had heard enough, and I was feeling embarrassed, so I just wanted to pay the check and leave. But later I felt proud and rewarded by God because I had just saved a life.

Well, not long after, another deputy that I worked with, and was friends with, got into a foot pursuit with a known suspect, and he was shot multiple times, nearly causing him to lose his life. His trial ended up being as bad or worse than the actual shooting.

I left working narcotics in order to get a break for a while; however, I was finding that there were no breaks. Crime was bad and just kept getting worse. And so were all the tragedies and horrific things that would continue to happen around me.

There was a place in Orlando, Florida, located in one of the zones that we were working in the bike unit. It was called the Diplomat Center and had recently closed down. It was a beautiful center with a swimming pool and very nice landscaping. There had been tens of thousands of dollars in damage caused by vandals that had been occurring at the center. I decided to get the unit together and set up a stakeout at the center and try to catch the vandals responsible for the damage.

We were all set up, and it was getting late into the evening. I decided to go up to the local 7-11 and get the guys some coffee. While I was there, I ran into a fellow deputy and friend, Deputy John Creegan. He was working that zone in patrol and was getting coffee and baseball cards for his son. We talked for a few minutes about our Harleys, and we discussed possibly going riding the upcoming weekend. I left and headed back to the stakeout location.

An hour or so had passed, and a call came out over the radio. The call was in regard to a vehicle pursuit involving a stolen vehicle, and it was coming out of Sector 4 or the south trail as we used to refer to it as. Me and the rest of my unit headed towards the Interstate I-4 and Lee Rd. on-ramp because the pursuit was headed east on

I-4 towards our direction. I had a couple deputies stop all traffic trying to enter I-4 from Lee Rd. As I was running up the on-ramp, I saw Deputy Creegan's patrol car positioned on I-4 with his overhead emergency lights on. It appeared that Deputy Creegan was in the process of putting out stop sticks. Stop sticks are spike strips that when run over by a vehicle, they will puncture the tires.

I got on the radio and warned deputies that even though pursuing deputies were calling out their location, the pursued vehicle was likely to be way ahead of them. I no sooner said that, and I witnessed the suspect driving the stolen pursued pick-up truck with no headlights or taillights on drive past the on-ramp at an extreme high rate of speed and steer straight towards Deputy Creegan's patrol car. Then I saw something fly through the air towards the middle of the Interstate. As I ran further onto I-4, I could see Deputy Creegan laying under the guard rail between the eastbound and westbound side of I-4.

I got on the radio and called out officer down, and I informed dispatch that I needed rescue personnel immediately. What I had seen fly through the air was Deputy Creegan.

The Orange County Sheriff's Office helicopter had been assisting with the pursuit, so I requested assistance from them by airlifting Deputy Creegan. I instructed another deputy from my unit to stop all eastbound traffic on I-4 so we could set up a landing zone for the helicopter referred to as Chase.

I held Deputy Creegan's hand and talked to him, assuring him that he was going to be ok. He kept telling me that if he could just get up then he would be fine. I had to hold him down and keep him as comfortable as I could until rescue units arrived because I knew that his injuries were serious. Deputy Creegan told me that he was having problems breathing, so I unfastened his duty belt and unfastened his bulletproof vest in an effort to help him breathe better. He was fighting to stay alive, he refused to give up.

Rescue units got on scene, and they began assessing Deputy Creegan's condition. One of the paramedics asked me to help him hold Deputy Creegan down while he treated his badly injured leg.

The paramedics working up near Deputy Creegan's head said, "Code, we've lost him."

I thought, *No that can't be possible, I was just talking to him, he has to be ok.* Chase landed, and Deputy Creegan was placed into the helicopter. The Orange County Sheriff's Office watch commander ordered the use of deadly force.

The suspect driving the stolen truck was continuing to travel at a high rate of speed in a reckless manner on I-4 eastbound, jeopardizing the safety and lives of innocent victims and refused to stop or obey pursuing deputies' commands to pull over. And he had also just killed an Orange County deputy.

One of the pursuing deputies pulled alongside of the truck and again ordered the driver to stop. The driver made an obscene gesture towards the deputy, so the deputy fired his service weapon in his direction, striking the suspect, causing him to wreck the stolen truck. The suspect was taken into custody and ended up being paralyzed as a result of his injuries. He died several years later.

Medical personnel told me that Deputy Creegan was so severely injured as a result of being hit by the truck, that he could not have ever survived. Deputy Creegan left behind a wife and children. He served honorably in the United States Navy and retired as a Master Chief Petty Officer after serving eighteen years. Deputy Creegan was able to retire early due to the closure of the Naval Training Center in Orlando, Florida, where he had been stationed. He had been with the Orange County Sheriff's Office for a short time and was serving the citizens of Orange County, Florida, honorably.

When I attended John's funeral, his son, Chris, wanted to meet with me in private. We discussed John's last words and how much of a fighter he was. Chris was just thirteen years old, and he admired his father. It was one of the most difficult moments in my life.

I returned to the scene of the accident with John's family and other members of the Orange County Sheriff's Office. While we there, Chris found one of John's ink pens and the baseball cards that John had bought for him. It was like John spoke to him. It was very touching and spiritual.

Once again, another moment in my life that I just happened to be there and cannot explain why.

I disliked stop sticks from the moment we first began training with them. I always thought that the focus was keeping everyone else safe; however, there was total disregard for the safety of the officer involved. I felt that there had to be a better way. Once a vehicle at a high rate of speed hits stop sticks, it can be thrown out of control, and you were still endangering the public. And on that evening, there was no way that Deputy Creegan could have gotten out of the way of a truck traveling at 100 miles per hour.

I also had a dislike for the Taser when we began training with that. I will explain why. We had a young deputy that engaged in a foot pursuit of a violent suspect. He caught up with the bad guy and struggled with him. The bad guy continued to resist, so the deputy tased him. As soon as the Taser completed its cycle, the bad guy pulled a real gun and shot the deputy. The deputy was paralyzed for the rest of his life. And at the time of the incident, he was only in his twenties. He could no longer perform the duties of a deputy sheriff, and not only were his usable legs taken from him, but so was the career he had chosen and loved.

Well, I didn't stay in the bike unit much longer because I was asked to go back to working narcotics. I transferred back to the Orange County Sheriff's Office street drug unit as an assistant supervisor. I was still actively working drug cases, buying crack cocaine, ecstasy, marijuana, and heroin.

One evening, I made a purchase of six grams of heroin from a guy in east Orlando, Florida. When the arrest team moved in to take him into custody, he fled in his car. We began to pursue him; however, we called off the pursuit as to not place any innocent victims in danger, and we let the Orange County Sheriff's Office helicopter follow him from overhead. The bad guy crashed his car into a telephone pole shortly after the pursuit began. He got out and fled into a heavily wooded area. We went to the scene of the crash and set up a perimeter. The helicopter was equipped with a thermal imaging camera that had the ability to pick up heat. The pilot could see the bad guy covering himself with what we later found to be wet leaves, and he was slowly disappearing from the camera. We had a canine deputy come to where we were, and he released his dog. The dog found the bad guy in no time at all. The bad guy should have come out when he was told to. He was arrested and treated by medical personnel that were on scene.

And now after this, I would again find myself in another very dangerous situation. I just couldn't seem to get a break. I was driving to where we would be executing a search warrant. The car that I was driving was a new Pontiac Formula with 700 miles on it. It was very sporty with a big engine and allowed me to sway drug dealers during undercover operations. I had another deputy in the car with me who was cross training with the drug unit. He had an interest in becoming an agent.

We were sitting at a red light, and I looked in my rearview mirror, and I saw a large white van coming up behind us at a high rate of speed. I said to the deputy with me that I didn't think that guy was going to stop. Like a parent would for some reason, I put my hand out over the deputy's chest to protect him, and I accelerated hard in an effort to eliminate some of the impact.

The Firebird broke traction due to all the horsepower, and the van hit us doing about fifty miles per hour. The impact knocked us all the way through the intersection and into the grassy medium. There was smoke and debris again, and it felt like something came through my lower back and out my lower abdomen. I asked the deputy with me to feel behind my seat and make sure nothing was stabbing me. He said that there wasn't. It must have just been extreme pressure from the impact. I later found that it caused a lower abdominal hernia.

My supervisor, Bruce, came to the scene, rescue personnel, and a Florida Highway Patrol Trooper. When they were putting me on the stretcher this time in order to transport me to the hospital, the man that hit me wanted a moment to say something to me. What he said was, "I just wanted to apologize."

I said, "It's ok, that's why they call it an accident."

He said, "No, I am sorry for wrecking that beautiful car that us taxpayers paid for."

I was trying hard to get off that stretcher, but my supervisor helped rescue personnel hold me down. The trooper did inform me though that the guy would be held accountable for the accident.

I was just in disbelief as to what the guy had said. He had no concerns whatsoever about my condition or about his actions and negligence involving the wreck. He was definitely a part of the problem with people today and not the solution. He must have just been another cop hater and someone that doesn't believe in the laws of the country. And by the way, that car wasn't paid for by taxpayers. It was paid for by illegal drug dealers. The money came from cash made by the dealers that had been seized and forfeited by the courts. I survived all that with injuries I would have to recover from, and I would have to move on.

An opening occurred in the Drug Enforcement Administration's Orlando, Florida, district office, so I put in for it. I was selected, so now I would become a DEA drug task force agent working federal drug cases. I started digging right away and hit the bricks running my first day. I had information about a guy that was part of a case that I had worked in MBI and brought that case with me.

I was a member of the DEA drug task force for about two years. During that time, I worked numerous drug cases that I had put together, and I testified before the federal grand jury multiple times. In every case, there was a successful outcome with the prosecution.

The DEA agents learned about the unusual things that often seemed to follow me and would joke about it. One day, everyone was going to lunch, and they refused to go with me because of it. I was in a restaurant eating by myself, and a man in the restaurant began having a grand mal seizure. Nobody seemed to know what to do, so I stepped in to help. The man was sitting in a booth, and because of the seizure, he was stiffening up, and I couldn't get him out of the booth. I was forced to break the table away from the wall that it was attached to so that I could make him comfortable on the floor. I placed my jacket under his head and made sure his airway was open and that he could breathe.

While I was tending to him, I told someone to call 911. A woman kept interjecting herself and telling me to stick his wallet in his mouth so that he didn't swallow his tongue. She was very distracting, and I finally said to her, "Please, go stand in the corner and try to swallow your tongue. It is impossible."

And then of all things, who do you think walked in during all this? The DEA agents from the office that I worked in. The ones that said they didn't want to go to lunch with me because of strange things happening around me. They looked down at me and just shook their heads. The man came out of the seizure, and he was ok. He was just a little embarrassed. What could I say about all this other than it happened again?

I remember one case that I assisted with while I was in the unit. It was a marijuana smuggling case out of Mexico, and the bad guys were living in Deland, Florida. I was assigned as part of the search warrant entry team that would be executing the warrant at the residence. We held a briefing in a parking lot in Deland in the early morning hour and were going to make entry into the house before sunrise.

We knocked and announced police numerous times, and there was no response at the door. We made forced entry and got inside. Once we were in the house, A DEA special agent continued to shout "Police with a search warrant." I could hear people scurrying in a bedroom, and the door was locked.

DEA special agents were about to crash the door, and I said, "Wait." I thought to myself, *At the briefing, I was told that these people were out of Mexico,* and I thought that they may not speak English.

I shouted, "*Abre la puerta, manos arriba, policia.*" Which means "Open the door, hands up, police."

The door came open, and there were several Mexican males in the room with their hands up. There was a gun in the closet that one of them was going to get. After speaking to them, we found that they didn't speak English, and they thought that it was a home invasion by other drug dealers after being awakened so early.

I sure got a funny look from full-time DEA agents when I blurted that out. They looked at me as if to be saying, "Where did that come from?" The absolute funny thing was that DEA special agents are sent to language school to learn Spanish, and none of them thought of using it. I speak very little Spanish, but what little I did know sure came in handy that morning.

This could have turned into a shoot-out and without reason. I am not trying to belittle anyone there that night, but I will again emphasize the importance of common sense and being on your toes in police work. Training is of the utmost importance too.

By my having worked at the state and local level for so many years, I dealt with bad guys on a daily basis. In DEA's defense, they do not encounter bad guys as frequent. Their cases are mostly more complex and lengthy.

Another case that I can think of while I was assigned to that office was a case again where they wanted to use me on the entry team. They had a guy that was supposed to be in a house, and he was wanted for drug charges and murder. I don't like to interject in other people's cases, but I just had to because I thought lives would be placed in jeopardy. I made a suggestion to instead of making a forced entry for me to place the Orange County Sheriff's Office SWAT Team on standby because they constantly train for this kind of entry. I also suggested that I call my Orange County communications center and obtain the phone number for the residence. Then we could call into the home and tell the bad guy that the house was surrounded and he needed to come outside and kneel in the front yard with his hands on his head.

They agreed with me. I made the call, and the bad guy came out and surrendered without any kind of incident. This was another case where common sense and quick thinking saved someone from a possible shooting. It was also a case where people put their heads together and came up with the best solution. It was big of them to have listened to me.

During another case that I was assisting DEA with in the Winter garden, Florida, area, two DEA special agents were standing in the street with a female. She had just arrived, and she was one of their suspects that they had federal charges on. I was sitting in my vehicle acting as a cover agent observing the surroundings. The two DEA agents were attempting to place handcuffs on the female when a male subject came running out of a house with about a four-foot pipe raised over his head, and he was running towards the two agents, going to attack them. I jumped out of my SUV and began running towards the male with the pipe. As I was running, I saw that one of the DEA agents saw him coming and was caught totally by surprise. The agent attempted to draw his gun, but he stumbled backwards. I tackled the male with the pipe and secured the weapon that he had. I found out from the male's grandmother that even though he was six feet tall and 175 pounds, he was only fourteen years old. She also told me that he was mentally handicapped and that the female the agents were arresting was his mother. I took a moment to gather my thoughts. I was banged up from hitting the concrete, but in thinking, I just saved a child from being shot, and it was a very good feeling. I received an award for my actions; however, it wasn't as rewarding as saving a life or preventing agents from being injured or killed.

Please don't misinterpret what I am saying as bragging. I am merely writing about facts of actual incidents that I was involved in. I never believed in big egos, and I can honestly say that I never had one. I have just always done things to the best of my ability and have always cared about a person's well-being. Being that of good guys or bad guys.

DEA has outstanding agents that have placed their lives in danger for years serving the American people. Some I considered friends, and I was very proud to have been able to serve the American people with them. There have been DEA special agents that have lost their lives in the line of duty, and they will never be forgotten.

Since I am talking about honoring law enforcement officers, I would also like to recognize Immigrations Customs Enforcement, Border Patrol, Bureau of Alcohol, Tobacco, and Firearms, the Federal Bureau of Investigation, the Secret Service, the Division of Alcoholic Beverage and Tobacco, and the Florida Department of Law Enforcement.

I have personally worked with members of each one of these agencies throughout my law enforcement career, and I can't express how honored I feel to have been able to do so. These agencies, too, have lost agent lives at the hands of criminals while serving the American people. Working with all the members that I have in law enforcement, I have never witnessed or been involved in any mistreatment of a suspect at any time and especially never witnessed mistreatment due to their race.

Getting back to the major case that I brought to DEA with me. I was trying to move forward with that case, however, couldn't get the resources to do so. In the best interest of relations between the Orange County Sheriff's Office and DEA, I requested a transfer.

The sheriff agreed to move me back into MBI where I could proceed with the case. Overall, I worked the case for approximately six years. It was a case out of Orlando that took me to Las Vegas, Nevada. I have written a book about it, titled *It $tayed in Vega$*.

After I returned to MBI, I managed to work the case to success and at the same time went through the promotional process and was promoted to sergeant.

Even working in my role as a narcotics supervisor, I remained active in initiating and working drug cases. I was the only supervisor to do so. I became a member of the FBI task force in MBI and was a part of that unit for two years.

I initiated a case involving a trucker that was bringing a load of cars out of Arizona. The trunk of one of the cars was full of marijuana. I met with the trucker in a parking lot in Ocoee, Florida, posing as the person taking delivery of the loaded car. We ended up arresting the trucker without a problem. I received MBI Agent of the Month for working that case.

Between my putting together drug cases and performing my duties as a supervisor, I was tasked with many other things. I was acting narcotics commander and also acting MBI director.

I wrote and managed a $100,000 federal grant that was utilized to fund a major drug case operation. I was responsible for keeping track of and documenting all expenditures.

On one occasion, the director came to me and said that the Orange County Sheriff's Office was being sued by a defendant and that I was assigned to investigate the case. I was told that I would be working directly with the sheriff's attorney. Once again, I don't know why this was being dropped in my lap, but it was. I worked the investigation for about eight months and was able to prove that the defendant's complaint had no merit. As a result of the investigation, we were able to get the case dismissed.

As you can see, working illegal narcotics in whatever unit you may have been assigned to can take up a better part of your life. So can police work in general. I started out living off a pager, for those of you old enough to remember, then went on to living off a cellular phone. It was a twenty-four-hour, seven-days-per-week job. I slept on picnic tables in rest areas on the Florida Turnpike waiting for large shipments of drugs coming out of Miami, Florida. I slept in parks waiting for bad guys to open packages of drugs that were delivered to their homes. Informants would call all hours of the night. If you did get time to spend with family, your time was always interrupted. Even the times I was able to take my family to Disneyworld, I would be interrupted there. It was very trying on family life and most would end up in divorce.

I retired from drug work and took a little break for a while. I returned to police work for a short time, I guess around ten months, and went to work as a police officer at an airport in the Orlando, Florida, area. I recalled on one occasion a flight being delayed. Everyone on that flight had already passed through TSA security, so we had to keep them all in another secure area until the other aircraft arrived to have them board. There was a Mexican family in that group, and the mother had a small infant. She expressed to me that she ran out of formula and diapers for her baby and that the baby was wet and hungry. She also told me that she didn't have any money. I was able to get out and get to a local store while they waited with other security personnel. I bought her some diapers and formula, and when I gave the items to her, you would have thought that I just bought her a new house. She was very thankful and emotional.

I only hope that through all the sacrifices made by the spectacular people that I have had the privilege to work with, it made some kind of difference in making a better life for the American people. America will never experience the type of protection that they received from the police in the previous years. Many improvements have been made over the years; however, many things have been taken away from the police that should not have. Law enforcement's hands are being tied more and more each year, and the streets have been given to the criminals These have been decisions made by politicians, and the public will be suffering as a result of it.

Let's talk about the terrorist attack on the federal building in Oklahoma City, Oklahoma. One hundred sixty-eight people lost their lives, including nineteen children. Six hundred and eighty people were injured. That occurred in 1995 at the hands of Timothy McVeigh. It was brave police that took that terrorist off our streets.

There are so many great cops in this country and throughout the world that have been willing to sacrifice so much for you. As I said before, they ran into burning towers while others ran out; they saved the citizens in Boston, and eventually, it would have been New York from the Boston Marathon bombers. They have been judged by citizens and by politicians. There have been protesting and demonstrating over bad police behavior in the US. The protesting turned into rioting and looting as a result. Are these actually true protests or an excuse to loot? There are bad cops, I've shown that throughout my story. The extreme majority are good.

In each instance that a cop involved death has occurred, the victim was committing a crime. Am I making an excuse for the death? Absolutely not. Every death is a tragedy. However, do these cop-related deaths give people the right to murder innocent police officers or injure and abuse innocent people? What makes the killers any better than the bad cop? In each case of every alleged allegation of police brutality, the suspect involved was in the commission of a crime and had resisted or attempted to injure the cop. If they had followed the officer's orders to comply, they would still be alive today. The tragic mishaps would never have happened. If the police were wrong in the handling of the incident, their agency could have been sued for the abuse, and the suspect would be a wealthy person as a result of the officer's inappropriate behavior.

Look into the number of corrupt politicians that have existed and still exist. Should they have immunity from legal action? These are the same people slandering good police officers. People judging cops that have never put on a badge or even have a clue as to what a police officer faces. Politicians tell you what you want to hear and not truth in order to get votes. Yet American people continue to vote for these corrupt people. They are fighting to defund our police departments across this nation. The same police that protect us from the violent criminals that lurk throughout our communities. Yet these same politicians will vote themselves a raise in salary whenever they see fit. And that is without the approval of the American people. These are the same people with security details. Why would they have to worry about police protection? They are the same people with walls around their houses and security gates.

Look into the number of people in the medical profession that are guilty of medical malpractice cases as I talked about earlier. Hundreds of thousands per year. And all that just for money. I will give you one final example of what I am talking about.

There was a cancer doctor, a hematologist, that came to the United States from Lebanon to practice medicine. He practiced in the state of Michigan. His name was Dr. Farid Fata. He was treating numbers of patients for cancer and administering large doses of chemotherapy. Some of his patients didn't even have cancer. He was overmedicating just for monetary gain. He was billing Medicare, Blue Cross Blue Shield, and other insurance companies for millions of dollars owed to him for the extreme dosages. He was actually killing American people to pay for his very expensive taste. He lived in a six-thousand-square-foot mansion. He was looking at purchasing a castle in Lebanon. He would have continued his malicious way of treating patients had it not been for a registered nurse that came to work at his office.

The nurse began watching closely how the patients coming to the office were being mistreated and receiving much longer doses of chemo than they required. They would sit in chairs for hours when they may have only needed fifteen-minute sessions. She knew that it was not right due to her nearly twenty years of experience as a nurse.

The nurse wrote a letter to the medical board basing a formal complaint about Dr. Fata's way of practicing medicine. The nurse waited a year before getting a response back. In the return letter, the response was that they found no improper behavior demonstrated by the doctor.

Well, after patient's family members began to become suspicious and the nurse's persistence regarding the doctor's wrongdoings, law enforcement got involved. Through the investigation, it was found that Dr. Fata had given chemotherapy to 553 patients that did not have cancer. He submitted thirty-four million dollars in fraudulent claims to Medicare and private insurance companies. The end result for Dr. Fata was that he received a forty-five-year prison sentence. One can only hope that he would never be allowed to practice medicine again.

All this intentional killing by a medical doctor, someone that a person places their life in the hands of, and not one word of the defunding of medical care. And a great deal of that money actually belonged to the American taxpayer when he defrauded Medicare. The ironic thing was that I have never had a doctor put his life on the line for me, such as police do often. There are doctors that save lives, but they don't put theirs at risk to save ours.

And after all this corruption for fortune and fame, not one protest by the people, not one riot, no looting, and no burning of buildings. The bad behavior was quickly forgotten. The doctor was punished for his wrongdoings, but does his punishment fit the crime? He took lives from family members that they can never get back. And he did it intentionally and for monetary gain. Not while fighting to save himself or someone else during a violent act against him.

There is talk about defunding police and replacing them with social workers. Well, having worn a badge and experiencing the real streets and not the make-believe streets that are told to you by Politicians, I say good luck with that plan. I only pray for the safety of the social workers being thrown into that mix.

As you can see, I have shared with you a great deal of facts and some of my opinions about police work and the political arena. I feel it is that of the people that believe in our laws and abide by our laws that back and support our police. I feel that the media continues to refuse to call the protesting or demonstrations that continue to occur across the country, riots, or looting. Instead they are referring to them as peaceful protests. The definition of a peaceful protest is a nonviolent resistance or nonviolent action, it is the act of disapproval through a statement or action without violence.

The first Amendment of the Constitution says that Congress shall make no law respecting an establishment of religion or prohibiting the free exercise thereof, or abridging the freedom of speech or of the press, or the right of the people PEACEABLY to assemble, and to petition the government for a redress of grievances.

I completely fail to understand how the media can compare the rioting, burning of buildings, looting, injuring and murdering numbers of police, injuries to innocent victims, or destruction of federal buildings to peaceful protests. People continue to be afraid to call it what it is. And I feel all of it was politically motivated just for votes.

The political figures in Portland, Oregon, criticized the president for sending in federal agents to assist in stopping the attacks on the Federal Courthouse in Portland. Police, state, local, and federal agents take an oath to protect people and property. It was obvious that the state politicians were trying to prevent the agents and their state and local police from honoring that oath. There were fireworks, Molotov cocktails, full canned goods, bottles, rocks, frozen eggs, and numerous other objects being thrown at agents, injuring several. There were lasers with extreme power being shined in the agents' eyes by the mob that were so powerful some agents suffered from blindness.

Those agents were doing their jobs by protecting a federal building. The rioters were even trying to destroy the fence that was erected to protect the building. I watched a great deal of coverage about the alleged peaceful protest on television and on the Internet. The media showed a lot of coverage that was quite different than what I had observed on the Internet. This was a riot, and there was nothing peaceful about it. Then the city of Portland threatened to fine the federal government for having the fence up. What outrageous, insane behavior demonstrated by the rioters and the local politicians. And what was the riot really about? What were they really protesting, and the main thing was, what were they accomplishing? There wasn't anyone in Portland that did anything to anyone of them prior to their unruly behavior. This was all about a bad cop in an entirely different state that will be held accountable if he is guilty of the crime against him. And if he is not, then that would be up to the courts to decide after they weigh all the evidence in the case.

There was a cop in Georgia that was charged for the murder of a suspect that he and another officer was attempting to arrest. The suspect fought with the two officers, and he was able to take the officer charged with murders Taser. The suspect turned and ran, and as he was running, the officer pursued him on foot. The suspect turned back towards the officer, and he fired the Taser at him. The officer allegedly fired his handgun, striking the suspect in the back, killing him. There was a great deal of criticism about the officer's actions by the public and the media.

My opinion regarding what happened was this. First of all, the suspect had committed several crimes leading up to the shooting. Were those crimes serious enough to use deadly force? Not until the suspect stripped the officer of his Taser and then he used it against him. A Taser was considered by the courts in different cases as a deadly weapon. It has been declared that people have died after being tased. In addition to that, had the officer been struck by the electrode prongs from the Taser, he would have been incapacitated, and the suspect could have taken his gun and used that against him. Another thing to consider was that by law, a law enforcement has no obligation to retreat.

There was also question as to why the police officer had to shoot the suspect in the back. It was my understanding that when the officers encountered the suspect, he had only initially committed a misdemeanor offense of DUI (driving under the influence). When the suspect resisted the way that he did, it would have made the officers wonder what other serious offense he may have committed that they weren't aware of.

The suspect was also fleeing with the officers Taser that could have been used as a deadly weapon on an innocent person. He could have carjacked somebody, or he could have entered someone's home and held them against their will in order to escape. An officer has an obligation to protect the general public, and had the officer let the suspect escape, the general public would have been in danger.

I will give you an example of an incident where a suspect got away due to a strict vehicle pursuit policy that was put into place to protect the public. That policy actually caused two innocent people to lose their lives.

You see, a police agency was in pursuit of a suspect from one municipality, and the pursuit was called off due to the strict policy. The suspect entered another municipality and abandoned the vehicle that he was driving. He encountered two innocent people at their home, and he beat them to death with a baseball bat. There was a ten-year-old boy present during this tragic ordeal. Could their horrific deaths have been prevented? I believe so.

There is one other thing that I would like to address. When I was in police work, numerous times I encountered bad guys that would make threats towards my family in an attempt of retaliation. They would tell me that they knew where I lived and that they would hurt my family. I said, and I meant what I said! I told them that if they ever came within a mile of my house, I would shoot them. I also told them that my family meant far more to me than the job. And believe me, I did mean it.

My family members had nothing to do with the arrests that I made in police work or the bad guys that I had to deal with. They should in no way have ever been included in any of it.

I can remember during my career in law enforcement, and even after, several incidents where an act of violence did occur at the homes of law enforcement officers, judges, lawyers, and their families. Innocent family members were injured or killed. And that is not acceptable. Our law officials should have protection from that kind of behavior, by at minimum keeping their residences private from the public. That information should not be public record.

We have sports figures, celebrities, and movie stars constantly giving their opinions or discontentment about the way our country is being run and about our police. They are all paid big money for what they do and are living very successful and lavish lifestyles. I feel that they should focus on their chosen careers and set an example for the common people and the children that look up to them. They are not subjected to the violence in the country, and if they are, most have their own security teams to protect them.

There are a lot of changes going on in America. When I grew up, American people wanted to work and provide for their families. Now, today's America seems to want to be dependent on their government and demand free things, instead of feeling the self-pride that it took to earn them.

I have provided a great deal of information about my career, my personal life, and that of the lives of other law enforcement officers. I did so in an effort to show that cops are human beings that come from all walks of life. They risk their lives on a daily basis in an effort to protect the American people. All the American people, regardless of sex, skin color, or ethnic background. They work at the state and local level as well as the federal level. They are not perfect, but if they were, they would be considered programmed machines and not human. I also showed that there was a great deal of other imperfect people in numerous positions throughout our country. They, too, are human beings.

I will yet add another example of bad behavior in law enforcement caused from the stresses of the job. The Secret Service that is made up of elite special agents who go through rigorous training had also suffered embarrassment on occasions.

Under the Obama Administration, during a summit being held in Cartagena, Colombia, in 2012, Secret Service special agents became part of a prostitution scandal. After an investigation was completed, the special agents lost their jobs.

Such a shame for something like that to happen. It takes a great deal to become a Secret Service special agent. Only one percent of applicants are accepted to process for the position. The hiring process on average takes twelve months. You would undergo a polygraph exam, extensive background check, employment activity check, financial status check, drug usage check, and your family members were even interviewed.

Once the agent is accepted, he or she would be sent to the Glynco training facility for three months of training. Then they were sent to the Maryland facility for eighteen weeks for additional training. For a Secret Service special agent to even be considered for the presidential protection detail, they would have to have been working in investigations for six years. And then they go through more training in defensive driving, protection and rescue procedures, and using their bodies as a shield to prevent harm from the president.

Through the years, special agents have suffered due to alcoholism and suicide due to the extreme stresses that the job produces. Those agents spend unthinkable time away from family and work hours on end without time off. You must also take into consideration that they are willing to take a bullet and risk their lives to protect the person they are assigned to protect. I think all considered, it should be expected that somewhere along the line, somebody would slip and make a mistake. But again, let's realize that when they did, they were held accountable. I still have respect for each and every one of them and honor the jobs they perform.

The critical thing is that regardless of positions, the behavior of all those people has to be closely monitored, and the bad people must to be held accountable for their crimes.

Our society has become so lopsided that the police are being abused and the criminals are being rewarded. You cannot function as a civilized nation with that type of mindset. The lives, property, and well-being of innocent people are at stake.

I will end by saying that I have so much pride and confidence in our police and our US Military. These are the people that protect our country and risk their lives for our freedom. I believe that I have shown that cops are people. Again, people from all walks of life and different backgrounds who make daily sacrifices by placing their lives on the line, and they continually miss out on quality family time. They deserve our appreciation, our support, and respect.

May God bless them all, protect them, and God bless America.

ABOUT THE AUTHOR

Rodney LeMond served twenty-eight years in law enforcement working at the state and local level, as well as working criminal cases at the federal level. During his tenure in police work, Rodney worked several high-profile drug cases and numerous other criminal cases throughout his law enforcement career. During that time, Rodney encountered numbers of unusual events that occurred and could not be explained. His childhood was not a glamorous one, and he went through many struggles growing up. Rodney will attempt to educate you as to the trials of being a cop in this country and what it takes to become a cop. He will also show you through his experiences in police work that cops are human beings and not programmable machines. Rodney will also talk about the good cops whom are the vast majority of cops and the few bad cops that are weeded out and punished. You will see that cops come from all walks of life and work hard for little pay, they make huge sacrifices, and all in order to serve the public. You will learn how administrators and politicians are tying the hands of police officers and preventing them from doing the job they took an oath to do. Here is the story of *You Can't Judge a Cop by Its Cover.*